THE
WARREN BUFFETT
STOCK PORTFOLIO

THE
WARREN BUFFETT
STOCK PORTFOLIO

Warren Buffett Stock Picks:
Why and When He Is Investing in Them

MARY BUFFETT & DAVID CLARK

**SIMON &
SCHUSTER**

London · New York · Sydney · Toronto · New Delhi

A CBS COMPANY

First published in Great Britain by Simon & Schuster UK Ltd, 2012
A CBS COMPANY

1 3 5 7 9 10 8 6 4 2

Simon & Schuster UK Ltd
1st Floor
222 Gray's Inn Road
London
WC1X 8HB

www.simonandschuster.co.uk

Simon & Schuster Australia, Sydney
Simon & Schuster India, New Dehli

A CIP catalogue for this book is available
from the British Library.

ISBN: 978-0-85720-842-2

Printed and bound by CPI Group (UK) Ltd, Croydon, CR0 4YY

For Miranda

And for Hunter

Contents

INTRODUCTION

In these very turbulent times we think it is best to start with a quote from Warren Buffett during the 1990–1991 recession:

> Nevertheless, fears of a California real estate disaster similar to that experienced in New England caused the price of Wells Fargo stock to fall almost 50% within a few months during 1990. Even though we had bought some shares at the prices prevailing before the fall, **we welcomed the decline because it allowed us to pick up many more shares at the new panic prices.**
>
> Investors who expect to be ongoing buyers of investments throughout their lifetimes should adopt a similar attitude toward market fluctuations; instead many illogically become euphoric when stock prices rise and unhappy when they fall.

Warren has always maintained that the time to buy stocks is when nobody else wants them. In the recession of 2008–2009 we had that opportunity, and for those of us who did venture into that abyss, the rewards were tremendous. As we look toward the end of 2011 and the beginning of 2012, we are once again seeing stock prices at price-to-earnings-ratios that we haven't seen since the early eighties. Coca-Cola is trading at 16 times earnings; in 1999 it was trading at 47 times earnings. The powerhouse Wal-Mart is trading at a P/E of 12; in 2001 it was trading at a P/E of 38. Procter & Gamble is selling at a P/E of 16; in 2000 it was trading at a of P/E 29. What does this mean?

As we enter the fifth year of what many economists are calling the Great Recession, we are finding that some of the most amazing businesses—those with fantastic long-term economics working in their favor—are trading at prices and price-to-earnings ratios that offer investors real opportunities for increasing their wealth. We aren't talking about opportunities for quick profit. We are talking about serious long-term moneymaking with ten-year compounding annual rates of return conservatively in the 8%–12% range. That is what the market is now offering us. Pessimism about the banking situation in Europe and the unemployment in the United States have created the perfect storm to bring stock prices down and offer value-oriented investors some great opportunities.

In our book *Warren Buffett and the Interpretation of Financial Statements* we focused on examining a company's financial statements to discover whether or not it has what Warren calls a "durable competitive advantage," which shows us if a company has great long-term economics working in its favor. In this book, we are looking only at companies that Warren has already identified as having a durable competitive advantage. These are the companies that he has bought for himself and for his holding company, Berkshire Hathaway, as long-term investments. Because of the recession, these companies are once again selling at prices that offer great long-term growth prospects.

Our primary concern is with teaching you how to value companies so you can create a conservative projection as to the kind of future return that an investment offers at its current market price. In Warren's world, as stock prices decrease, the prospects for the investment increase. Putting a number on those prospects tells us whether or not the stock is an attractive buy.

We start with a brief history of Warren's investment strategy and then explain how to interpret a company's per share earnings and per share book value histories. This allows us to quickly identify a company with a durable competitive advantage and to project the compounding annual rate of return the investment offers. We then look closely at seventeen investments in Warren's current stock portfolio, working up a case study and valuation for each company. We also take a quick look at the investments made by Berkshire's other three investment managers.

Historically, we have reason to believe that our projections ten years out are accurate under normal business conditions. Throughout this book, we have kept the projections conservative.

When you are done with this book you should be able to quickly determine whether a company has a durable competitive advantage and whether or not the company's stock is attractively priced.

Presently there are four people at Berkshire Hathaway who are "picking stocks" for Berkshire's portfolio. On top is Warren Buffett, who makes 99% of the investment decisions for Berkshire. Then there is Charlie Munger, who often discusses investments with Warren and whose enthusiasm has put Berkshire into a few out-of-the-box investments. There are also newcomers Todd Combs, whom Warren hired in 2010 to help him pick stocks for Berkshire, and Ted Weschler, who will officially join Berkshire in early 2012 as a portfolio manager. The major portion of this book is concerned only with the companies that Warren Buffett has invested in personally and/or made the decision for Berkshire to invest in. At the end of the book, for those who are curious, we take a brief look at Charlie Munger's, Todd Combs's, and Ted Weschler's respective investment styles and the contributions they have made to Berkshire's portfolio.

So, without any more delay, let's begin our exploration into Warren Buffett's Stock Portfolio.

MARY BUFFETT & DAVID CLARK

CHAPTER 1

The History and Evolution
of Warren Buffett's Investment Strategy

Understanding Warren Buffett's investment genius is not that difficult. However, it is often counterintuitive to the investment theories and strategies that 99% of most investors follow. What is counterintuitive about Buffett's methods? Well, when others are rushing to sell off stocks, Warren will be selectively buying in. The key word here is "selectively." When Warren is buying in, he is picking the cream of the crop—companies that have a "durable competitive advantage."

And when the whole world is counting its riches after buying into a bull market, we find Warren selling out into the rising market, gathering a large cash position. In the two or three years that make up the top of a bull market, we are likely to find Warren sitting idly about—doing nothing—appearing to be missing all the easy money offered up by the seemingly endless rise in stock prices.

In fact, at the high end of the last two bull markets, investment pundits of the day pointed their fingers at Warren,

1

proclaiming he had lost his touch or was over the hill. Yet when these markets finally crashed, and the masses were bailing out of stocks, who did we find at the bottom of the investment barrel picking up some of the greatest companies in the world at bargain prices? Warren Buffett.

Buffett's early strategy was to cash out of the market when it started to reach a buying frenzy, as in the late sixties. In later years he simply stopped buying when prices got too high and let the cash build up in Berkshire Hathaway, waiting to take advantage of the inevitable crash in stock prices. It is his superior understanding of the microeconomic forces that drive individual businesses that allows him to pick future winners from the heap of rubble. He buys into companies that have superior long-term economics in their favor. These exceptional businesses make for superior long-term, twenty-to-forty-year investments.

When the stock market crashes, Warren buys into companies that have good economics working in their favor—companies he sells as the market and their stock prices recover. This gives him cash for future investments. He also invests in individual "events" that might—over the short term—drive down a company's share price below what its long-term economics makes it worth. And he is a big player in the field of arbitrage, which also generates large amounts of cash.

Buffett's key to success begins by having cash when others

don't. Then he waits. Once the stock market is crashing and offering up excellent businesses at bargain prices, he is in there buying. Next he holds on to the really great businesses as the market moves up, selling off the average businesses and letting the cash start to pile up. Finally, as the market starts to move onto high ground, he lets the excess income from dividends and stock sales pile up in his cash account— keeping only the companies with a durable competitive advantage that will help make him superrich over the long term. (Warren lets the cash income from all of Berkshire's businesses build up. Individual investors would let earned excess income accumulate in their money market account.)

Warren has repeated this cycle over and over and over again to the point that he has an enormous portfolio of some of the finest businesses that have ever existed, and in the process, he has become the third richest person in the world.

What this book will do for you as an investor is show you the companies that Warren has identified as having a long-term economic advantage and that he holds investments in today. It also shows you how to value the companies to help determine if the price you pay today—or sometime in the future—will give you an attractive rate of return.

Warren's Evolution from Short-Term Bargain Buyer to Long-Term Durable Competitive Advantage Investor

At the start of Buffett's career, he fell under the influence of the dean of Wall Street, Benjamin Graham, who developed what is known today as value investing. Graham was originally a bond analyst looking for undervalued situations in bonds. Graham then started applying his theories to common stocks—he identified "businesses" he thought the stock market was undervaluing, bought them, and held on to them for three years with the hope that the stock market would revalue them upward. However, in the crashes of 1929 and 1932, Graham was nearly wiped out. He stayed in the game, vowing to earn back the money he lost for his investors; and in the aftermath of the Great Depression, he found himself in a very fertile field of companies whose share prices had been decimated, but were once again on the mend.

The impact of the Great Depression on stock prices is now long forgotten, but what happened from 1929 to 1932 was that the Dow Jones Industrial Average (DJIA) lost approximately 88% of its value, falling from 380 to 43. If that were to happen today, we would be looking at a decline in the DJIA from 12,000 to around 1,500. The impact of the Great Depression was so powerful on stock prices that it wasn't until twenty-four years later—in 1956—that the DJIA once again returned to its 1929 high of 380.

The 1929 to 1932 fall in stock prices foreshadowed a destruction of the world economy unlike anything we have experienced since. Even good, strong businesses lost demand for their products. As they lost demand for their products, they laid off people and cut back production, sending the economy even deeper into a hole. As the economy started to improve, the stronger companies—makers of branded products—the ones that possessed some kind of durable competitive advantage, saw their stock prices improve a lot more quickly than the second- and third-tier companies. In fact, many of these second- and third-tier companies— smaller cap businesses that didn't have a durable competitive advantage—wouldn't see a resurgence in their stock prices until the bull markets of the fifties and sixties.

It is in the ranks of the second- and third-tier businesses, companies that most investors have never heard of, that Graham was able to really apply his trade, in the thirties, forties, and fifties, for these were the companies whose stock prices languished in the aftermath of the Great Depression. It was also in this second and third tier of business that Warren got his start investing in "Grahamian" bargains.

What happened was that after the 1929–1932 stock market crash, the larger, stronger, first-tier businesses that had durable competitive advantages made early economic comebacks, as did their stock prices. But the investing public as a whole, having lost a great deal of wealth in the great crash of 1929–1932, shied away from the stock market and became leery of second- and third-tier businesses. As time progressed these businesses did better, and some of them did really well, but their stock prices were slow to follow. It was not unusual for Graham literally to buy these companies for less than their book value. The businesses improved over time, but everybody ignored them—except for the likes of Graham. Warren saw Graham's kind of "value" investing as offering him the opportunity to "buy a dollar for fifty cents," and buy he did.

Warren practiced in this lucrative playing field for much of the fifties and sixties, poring over what were then called "pink sheets," which comprised a daily publication of stock quotes for second- and third-tier companies that traded over the counter. This was where Graham and Warren went looking for "bargains." As the stock market began once again to attract the individual investors who had fled en masse during the great crash, the prices on even the undervalued second- and third-tier stocks began to rise. This return of the "retail investor" in the sixties drove stock prices to new highs, making Warren and his investors rich.

In the late sixties, as the stock market rose higher and higher, Warren found less and less to buy. The pool of bargain second- and third-tier companies was starting to dry up. This meant that Warren was finding fewer opportunities to make money in the stock market. The days of being able to buy a dollar for fifty cents were over.

Something else bothered Warren. Not only was it harder to find undervalued companies to invest in, but also the stock market was reaching dizzying new highs. Popular consumer stocks like Avon were consistently trading at between 50 and 70 times earnings. Warren, a student of financial history, knew that this couldn't last forever, that eventually the bubble would burst and stock prices would come tumbling down. He also knew that getting out in a high market was the one thing that Graham had failed to do in the late 1920s. Graham had gotten caught up in the easy money of the 1920s bull market and had ridden it to the top and over the edge—losing significant amounts of money for himself and his clients. Graham was a genius at finding bargains, but he didn't know enough to walk away from the table when things got too hot.

In 1969 Warren did what Graham had failed to do in 1929: He cashed in his chips and walked away from the game. Warren closed down his investment partnership, gave his investors their significant profits, sold off his investment portfolio, turned it into cash, and then did nothing for three long years. As he has said, he "sat on his hands" while the rest of the investment community was making tons of easy money. As Buffett has often said, those were three of the longest years of his life, but he didn't budge—he stayed in cash.

Then, in early 1973, the speculation reached the peak of its madness, oil prices shot through the roof, interest rates went from 5% to 10%, and then it all quickly started to fall. Over the next year and a half, the Dow Jones industrial average benchmark lost over 45% of its value.

Warren got out of the market in 1969, but it is interesting to note that his friend and business associate Charlie Munger, who was running his own hedge fund at the time, stayed in, and made the same mistake Graham had made in 1929. The crash of 1973–1974 cost Munger's partners 53% of their investment. If you had had $1 million invested with Munger at the beginning of 1973, by the end of 1974 your holdings would have dwindled to $466,485. The experience was so horrifying to Munger that after the market started to come back in 1976, and he earned back for his partners part of the money he had lost, he shut down his hedge fund.

When the market crashed in 1973, and some of the greatest companies in America were being sold at bargain prices, Warren was literally "loaded for bear." As he has said about that period, "I felt like a sex-starved man in a harem." By the end of 1974 he was back in the market. But this time he wasn't buying Grahamian bargains; he was out after the good stuff, the companies that had a long-term durable competitive advantage—companies that would make him superrich over the long-term.

The late 1960s was when Warren started to realize that many of the Grahamian bargains he had been buying for fifty cents on the dollar were, as he has said, nothing more than discarded cigarette butts with no more than one or two puffs left in them—which made them lousy long-term investments. What he discovered was that the world of business was made up of two very distinctive business entities. There were companies with average to mediocre economics working in their favor—the vast majority of businesses, which made poor long-term investments. And there was a much smaller number of companies that had great business economics working in their favor, what Warren calls a long-term durable competitive advantage. It is this competitive advantage that allows them to produce superior results as businesses and for their investors over a long period of time.

In 1973 Warren was busy buying. But not the Grahamian bargain companies that he had bought in the past. He was buying companies that had a durable competitive advantage that, if held for a long period of time, would make him one of the richest people in the world.

When the crash of 1973 hit, Warren was buying shares of some of the best companies in America at bargain prices.

It was in 1973 that Warren acquired 1,727,765 shares in The Washington Post Company for $6.36 a share at a total cost of $11 million. Today that investment is worth approximately $616 million, which is a 5,500% increase in value and equates to an 11.17% compounding annual rate of return for 38 years—which would put a giant smile on any investor's face.

Now, There Is an Important Lesson to Be Learned Here

Warren got out of the market in 1969, when he felt that it was way overpriced, and he kept his investments in cash. Professional investors laughed at him as the market rose higher and higher. But when the market crashed in 1973 and 1974, Warren had more than enough cash to take advantage of the super-low prices on some really great companies.

2007—Déjà Vu All Over Again

Now let's shift to 2007. Warren thinks the market is too high and he is letting cash pile up inside Berkshire Hathaway to the tune of $37 billion, making it one of the most cash-rich companies in the world. Again, Wall Street professional investors were questioning his wisdom in being so "top loaded" with cash. But when the crash hit in 2008 and the major investment banks and financial institutions were falling like a house of cards, who did they turn to? The man with all the cash—Warren Buffett. He took Berkshire's cash and once again bought major positions in some of America's greatest businesses. These were the deals of a lifetime. Industrial giant General Electric sold Berkshire $3 billion worth of preferred stock, paying a 10% annual dividend and tossing in warrants for Berkshire to buy an additional $3 billion in GE common stock for $22.50 a share for five years. (Which means that Berkshire has an option to buy $3 billion worth of GE common stock at $22.50 a share until 2013.) Buffett cut a similar deal with Goldman Sachs, the most powerful investment bank in the world; he bought $5 billion in preferred stock that pays a 10% annual dividend, and he obtained an option to buy another $5 billion of Goldman Sachs's common stock at $115 a share. While these preferred deals were not open to us, Warren also made a deal with Swiss Re, the second largest reinsurance company in the world, for $2.5 billion in convertible preferred stock that paid a 12% annual rate of interest. While these preferred deals were not open to us, Warren was also busy snapping up shares in Burlington Northern (today BNSF Railway Co.) and Wells Fargo—which were. Many articles about Buffett's stock purchases say that he buys preferred stock on very generous terms, including long-lasting warrants to buy common stock at an attractive price. In fact, this is true of only a small portion of the investments he has made historically.

And where were all the value-investing devotees who worshipped at the temple of Benjamin Graham during the financial crisis in 2007? Losing money with everyone else, just as Benjamin Graham did in 1929 and 1932.

We'll get into the actual buying and selling dynamics later in the book, but remember, if Warren hadn't gotten out of the market completely in 1969, he too would have lost a large portion of his and his investors' money.

What we also want you to focus on is the fact that, in market crashes, Warren isn't buying the Grahamian bargains he cut his investing teeth on; instead, he is focusing on the exceptional businesses—the ones with a durable competitive advantage.

Now, This Is Important

Warren's investment philosophy is easy to understand. Build up a cash reserve and allocate it when prices are most in your favor. Warren does this on an individual company basis. He is not watching the market—he is watching the price of a company's stock, and he is keeping his eyes on a lot of different businesses. He gets his best prices in either a true bear market—as with the Washington Post Company; an industry recession—as with Wells Fargo; or a onetime event that decimates a company's stock—as with American Express.

What he wants to own are companies that have some kind of durable competitive advantage over their competition. He wants to own these companies for as long as possible and to buy them at the cheapest price possible. Which usually means during a bear market. Once Warren gets ahold of one of these super businesses, he'll hold the position as long as the underlying economics of the company don't change.

So the model is quite simple: Let the cash pile up, identify the companies with a durable competitive advantage, and then buy them in a down market—and hold them for the long term. Sounds easy, doesn't it? The problem is that most investors are preconditioned to buy in a bull market. This means they never have a stockpile of cash on hand, which means that when a bear market hits, they lose money, get upset, and then don't have the cash needed to take advantage of all the great prices.

As we said earlier, Warren's strategy is counterintuitive to what the rest of the market is doing—when others are selling, he is buying. When others are celebrating their bull market riches, he is socking cash away so he has plenty of financial firepower when the next bear market hits.

In a bear market or a panic, Warren uses his superior knowledge of business to buy into the companies that have superior long-term economics working in their favor.

If we follow Warren's investment strategy, we will find ourselves rushing into the market when others are rushing out. We find ourselves moving into cash as others are moving into stocks. We find ourselves being more price-sensitive, as opposed to market-sensitive. And all of this is made possible because we know WHAT to buy and WHEN to buy.

This book is about the WHAT to buy, and we have cheated a little—we are going to focus only on the companies that Warren has already identified as having a durable competitive advantage, the ones that are already in his portfolio. We are going to talk a little bit about the characteristics of the different companies and then we are going to show you how to value these companies, given their current market price. Using this information, you will be able to tell whether the company in question is or isn't an attractive investment. We are going to start with the little-known fact that Warren likes his companies old.

CHAPTER 2

Warren Likes His Companies Old

A long-term or durable competitive advantage in a stable industry is what we seek in a business.

WARREN BUFFETT

I look for businesses in which I think I can predict what they're going to look like in ten to fifteen years' time. Take Wrigley's chewing gum. I don't think the Internet is going to change how people chew gum.

WARREN BUFFETT

Warren has a saying, "Predictable products equal predictable profits," and it is the predictability of a company's profits that allows him to quickly figure out if the company has a durable competitive advantage or not. In determining predictability, one of the first things he does is look to see how old the products or services of the company are. A company that sells the same brand-name product or service for more than fifty years has a durable competitive advantage working in its favor.

When we look at Warren's stock portfolio, we see that it is filled with some very old companies selling some very old products and services. For example: Kraft's Nabisco Oreo cookie—America's best-selling cookie—has been on the market since 1912; Kraft itself has been in the packaged cheese game since 1903. American Express, a longtime Buffett favorite, started up in New York City back in 1850, and Wells Fargo, Warren's favorite bank, was founded in 1852. Coca-Cola was first sold in 1886. Procter & Gamble started selling soap in 1837, and Johnson & Johnson's surgical dressings hit the market in 1887. Pharmaceutical giant GlaxoSmithKline was the result of the merger of GlaxoWellcome, founded in 1880, and SmithKline Beecham, which opened its first pharmacy back in 1830. Wal-Mart and Costco are the young'uns in Warren's portfolio, with Wal-Mart getting its start in 1962 and Costco in 1983.

Why is OLD so important to Warren? It has to do with the product or service the company is selling. Take Coca-Cola for an example: Coke has been manufacturing and selling the same product for well over a hundred years. It spends very little on research and development and has to replace its manufacturing machinery only when it wears out. This means that the company gets maximum economic use out of its plants and equipment before it has to replace them.

Compare Coca-Cola to a company like Intel, which must spend billions every year on research and development just to stay competitive in its field. If it fails to spend the billions in R&D, then in three or four years' time the Intel computer processing chips it is selling will be outdated and useless. This is one of the reasons that Warren has stayed away from the computer industry no matter how good its stocks look— it changes too quickly and is difficult to understand. In the computer and software business the road ahead is never very clear, and if Warren can't see a long way down the road, he simply doesn't go there.

Old also goes to the nature of the product. Do you think that if Coke has been selling the same product for the last hundred years, it will be selling the same product ten or twenty years from now? Would you bet that children the world over will still be eating Oreo cookies fifty years from now? Warren is betting big that fifty years from now children will still be tearing their Oreo cookies apart, licking the icing off them, and dunking them in milk with the same gusto as they have for the last hundred years. And when they do, Kraft and Warren will be making money.

There is something else that is important about OLD— predictability of the earnings stream. Once a product like Coke gets established in a country, the earnings stream becomes fairly steady, and the company's income from its products has a certain predictability. For Warren the age of the company and the consistency of the company's earnings are good indications that the company has a durable competitive advantage working in its favor.

CHAPTER 3

Consistency in Earnings

A company that has a durable competitive advantage will show consistency in earnings over an extended number of years. This is reflective of the underlying economics of the business. Warren has discovered that companies that don't show a long-term consistency in earnings usually make poor long-term investments. Let's look at the ten-year earnings histories of the companies in Warren's stock portfolio of durable competitive advantage companies.

EARNINGS HISTORY

Warren has discovered that one of the primary identifiers of the company with a durable competitive advantage is an earnings history that shows a consistent and strong upward trend over a ten-year period.

He has also learned that if a company has an erratic earnings history, it is more likely the kind of company that produces what he calls a "commodity" type product, a product that has no brand identification and that competes in the marketplace solely on the basis of price. A perfect example would be lumber, but the class extends itself into airline flights; airlines tend to compete on price, with the cheapest seat winning. The second class of companies that have erratic earnings histories are companies that produce products that are constantly in need of upgrading and redesign to stay competitive with the competition. Here we have the whole class of high-tech companies that experience one boom and bust cycle after another.

Our company with a durable competitive advantage will have a ten-year earnings history that looks similar to these durable competitive advantage companies—Procter & Gamble, Coca-Cola, and Johnson & Johnson—that Warren has already invested in.

Procter & Gamble

From 2001 to 2011, Procter & Gamble increased its per share earnings by 155%, from $1.56 a share to $3.98 a share, with total per share earnings for the period of $30.78 a share. Now look closely at the company's per share earnings history. It shows great consistency and upward strength, which is what Warren is looking for. It's one of the signs of the presence of a durable competitive advantage.

Procter & Gamble's Earnings Per Share

Year	EPS ($)
'11	3.98
'10	3.53
'09	3.58
'08	3.64
'07	3.04
'06	2.76
'05	2.53
'04	2.32
'03	2.04
'02	1.80
'01	1.56

Coca-Cola

Now let's look at Coca-Cola: From 2001 to 2011, Coke increased its share price by 140%, from $1.60 to $3.85, with total per share earnings for the period of $27.52, which is very much a "bubbling upward" trend.

Coca-Cola's Earnings Per Share

YEAR	EPS ($)
'11	3.85
'10	3.49
'09	2.93
'08	3.02
'07	2.57
'06	2.37
'05	2.17
'04	2.06
'03	1.95
'02	1.65
'01	1.60

Johnson & Johnson

If we look at Johnson & Johnson, we can see, from 2001 to 2011, Johnson & Johnson enjoyed a 154% increase in earnings per share—from $1.91 to $4.85, never having a losing year and earning a total of $40.16 a share for the period, showing a very solid upward trend as well.

Johnson & Johnson's Earnings Per Share

Year	EPS ($)
'11	4.85
'10	4.76
'09	4.63
'08	4.57
'07	4.15
'06	3.76
'05	3.50
'04	3.10
'03	2.70
'02	2.23
'01	1.91

Now what I want you to focus on is not only the upward earnings trend that Procter & Gamble, Coca-Cola, and Johnson & Johnson have had but also to notice the consistency as well—a very steady rise, with never a down year.

Let's compare the earnings histories of several other big-name companies that are arguably commodity-type businesses: United Continental, the airline holding company; Ford Motor, the auto and truck manufacturer; and Advanced Micro Devices, the computer chip maker. All three of these companies sell products or services in markets where there is heavy competition from other manufacturers or service providers. In the face of such intense competition, their historic per share earnings picture is quite dismal. Which tells us that as businesses they lack any kind of durable competitive advantage that will result in increasing shareholders' wealth over a long period of time.

Let's take a look at them.

United Continental Holdings

From 2001 to 2011, United—a world-class airline with gross annual revenues of $36 billion—showed erratic earnings and managed to lose $107.65 a share during the ten-year period. This is an earnings history that you might wish on your worst enemy.

United Continental's Earnings Per Share

Year	EPS ($)
'11	4.75
'10	4.30
'09	-7.49
'08	-13.63
'07	2.32
'06	-0.16
'05	-4.88
'04	-9.87
'03	-15.20
'02	-34.56
'01	-33.23

Ford Motor Company

From 2001 to 2011, Ford also showed a very erratic earnings history—losing for its shareholders a total of $10.10 a share, which isn't as bad as United's, but not the kind of earnings history that sends the kids to college.

Ford Motor Company's Earnings Per Share

YEAR	EPS ($)
'11	2.00
'10	1.66
'09	0.86
'08	-6.50
'07	-1.43
'06	-6.72
'05	0.86
'04	1.59
'03	0.35
'02	0.19
'01	-2.95

Advanced Micro Devices, Inc.

From 2001 to 2011, Advanced Micro Devices, which competes with Intel in the design and sale of processing chips for computers, showed a very erratic earning history, with profits only four out of the ten years, and losses during this period of $11.92 a share.

Advanced Micro Devices, Inc.'s Earnings Per Share

YEAR	EPS ($)
'11	0.55
'10	0.64
'09	0.45
'08	-4.03
'07	-5.09
'06	-0.28
'05	0.37
'04	0.25
'03	-0.79
'02	-3.81
'01	-0.18

Now, as you read this today, without considering the price you pay, which companies do you think will make you richer in ten years' time? Is it Johnson & Johnson or United Continental Airlines? Coca-Cola or Ford Motor Company? Procter & Gamble or Advanced Micro Devices?

It's really not that hard to see the long-term economic benefit that a durable competitive advantage gives Johnson & Johnson, Procter & Gamble, and Coca-Cola. The trick is being able to identify these wonderful companies and then value them so we know whether the price we are paying is too high or is a bargain. One of the concepts that Warren uses in valuing these businesses involves his theory of the Equity Bond.

CHAPTER 4

The Warren Buffett Equity Bond

One of the great realizations Warren has had is that a company with a durable competitive advantage has earnings that are so predictable that its common stock "equity" is really a kind of "bond" with a variable coupon. He calls these equity bonds.

Bonds are debt securities sold by a company. Investors can buy a company's bond and earn a fixed rate of return. On a $100 bond that pays a fixed annual 10% rate of return, the investor would be paid $10 a year for the life of the bond. When the bond matures, the interest payments stop and the company pays the investor back his $100. Stocks, meanwhile, represent the company's equity and have variable earnings that depend on what the company earns in any given year. With bonds, the interest is fixed and certain; with earnings, there is great variability and with that variability in earnings comes a great deal of volatility in stock prices. Warren's revelation was that a company with a durable competitive advantage has such predictable earnings that the stock really is more like a bond—thus the name "equity bond." What makes these durable competitive advantage equity bonds so attractive is that the stock market periodically misprices them in relation to their worth as a long-term investment.

In Warren's world the "rate of return" on the "equity bond" is equal to what the company's net profits are in any given year. If the company stock has a per share book value of $100 a share and has annual after–corporate tax earnings of $8 a share, Warren would argue that the equity bond is producing an annual after–corporate tax return of 8%.

If the company has been growing its net earnings at a historical annual rate of 10%, then Warren would argue that his $100 equity bond is going to give him an initial rate of return of $8, or 8% ($8 ÷ $100 = 8%), and that that initial rate of return is going to grow at a projected annual rate of return of 10%. This means that as time goes on, the underlying return on the equity bond will increase.

Thus, the equity bond becomes an "expanding equity bond" because, over time, the rate of return on our initial investment keeps "expanding" as the company's pretax earnings continue to grow.

Now, if we can buy a Warren equity bond at its per share book value, which in this example is $100 a share, and it has net earnings of $8 a share, we can argue that we are earning an after–corporate tax return of 8%. But we seldom get to buy one of these great businesses at its per share book value. We normally have to pay a premium, which is embodied in the current market price for the company's shares. This means that a stock price higher than the per share book value will mean a lower rate of return. So, in our example, if the company's stock has a per share book value of $100 a share, but is selling for $150 a share in the stock market, and we spend $150 a share, our rate of return drops down from 8% to 5.3% (8 ÷ $150 = 5.3). At $150 a share, our $100 equity bond is going to produce a return of 5.3%. But wait, it gets more interesting.

Since we are dealing with a company with a durable competitive advantage whose per share earnings have been growing at a historic annual rate of 10%, Warren would argue that we just bought a $100 equity bond for $150, which will give us an initial rate of return of $8, which equates to 5.3%, and that initial rate of return will grow at a projected annual rate of 10%. As an investor, does that interest you?

Ten years from now, the $8 a share that we are earning in 2011, growing at 10% a year, will in theory grow to $20.75 a share in 2021. Which give us an after–corporate tax rate of return of 13.8% on our $150 per share investment ($20.75 ÷ $150 = 13.8%).

Does this work in real life?

In 1988 Warren, using his equity-as-a-bond theory, had Berkshire Hathaway buy 113.3 million Coca-Cola equity bonds (stock) at $5.22 a share. In 1988 Coca-Cola had a book value of $1.07 a share and net earnings of $0.36 a share; it also had a long history of consistent earnings growth. Warren figured that he was buying a Coca-Cola equity bond that was going to earn him a 6.8% initial rate of return (0.36 ÷ 5.22 = .068) and that his rate of return would increase over time as Coca-Cola's earnings increased, which would also increase the underlying value of the company and Coke's stock price. Jump to 2011: Berkshire still owns those 113.3 million Coca-Cola shares, but Coca-Cola is now earning $3.85 a share and is trading at $65 a share, giving Warren a 1,145% return on his 1988 investment of $5.22 a share, which equates to earning a compounding annual rate of return of 11.59% for twenty-three years.

Companies with a durable competitive advantage have the ability to grow their per share earnings over a long period of time. This causes an increase in their underlying intrinsic value, which over time the stock market will recognize. Warren has often said that as long as a company's fundamental economics are improving, he doesn't care if the stock price goes down on a short-term basis, because he knows that eventually the stock market will increase the share's market price to reflect the increase in intrinsic value.

CHAPTER 5

Projecting an Investment's Future Return

Let's start by running through a quick earnings analysis of Coca-Cola at its present 2011 price of $65 a share. If we look at Coca-Cola's earnings history for the last ten years, we can see the following:

Coca-Cola's Earnings Per Share

YEAR	EPS ($)
'11	3.85
'10	3.49
'09	2.93
'08	3.02
'07	2.57
'06	2.37
'05	2.17
'04	2.06
'03	1.95
'02	1.65
'01	1.60

The first step is just to take a look at the historic earnings picture. Is it showing consistent growth? Are there any years of loss? If so, why? Here we can see immediately that over the last sixteen years Coca-Cola has shown a consistent upward trend.

The next step is to measure that trend. To do this we have to pick a time period. Warren prefers using ten years' worth of historic numbers to get a good picture of the company. But if a longer earnings history is available he'll gladly use that as well.

Here we have an eleven-year history for Coca-Cola, which starts in 2001 and ends in 2011. In our calculation year 2001 is year zero and year 2002 is year one. To determine Coca-Cola's earnings growth rate from 2001 to 2002, we can use a rate of return function on a financial calculator or go to http://www.moneychimp.com/calculator/discount_rate_calculator.htm, which is a discount rate of return calculator found on the Internet. (Note: There are lots of financial calculators on the Internet and all are free.)

Plug in Coca-Cola's 2001 per share earnings of $1.60 as the Present Value; plug in the company's 2011 per share earnings of $1.65 as the Future Value, and plug in 1 for the Number of Years (it's one year from the end of 2001 to the end of 2002); then hit Calculate; we get 3.13%, which is the rate of growth for Coca-Cola's per share earnings for one year, from 2001 to 2002.

'02 $1.65 ← Future Value (Year One)

'01 $1.60 ← Present Value (Base Year)

Number of years: 1

Annual Rate of Growth: 3.13%

That is how it is done for one year. But to get a grip on Coca-Cola's long-term economic picture, we need to determine what the company's earnings growth rate is over a much longer period of time.

To do this, we plug in Coca-Cola's 2001 per share earnings of $1.60 as the Present Value; plug in Coca-Cola's 2011 per share earnings of $3.85 as the Future Value; and plug in 10 for the Number of Years; then we hit Calculate and get 9.18% as an annual rate of growth for the ten years.

'11 $3.85 ← Future Value (Year Ten)

'01 $1.60 ← Present Value (Base Year)

Number of years: 10

(Note: We need eleven years' worth of earnings to get a growth rate for a ten-year period. Remember, the Present Value Year is the base year and counts as zero. In this case, year 2001 would be year one and 2011 would be year ten.)

Annual Rate of Growth: 9.18%

Warren can argue that if he pays $65 a share for Coca-Cola's stock, he will be earning an after–corporate tax rate of return of 5.9% ($3.85 ÷ $65 = .059). Warren can also argue that this initial rate of return of $3.85 will grow over time at Coca-Cola's historical per share growth rate of 9.18%. Think of it as an expanding equity bond—where the interest rate on the bond expands over a period of time.

Now, this information will also allow Warren to project what Coca-Cola's per share earnings will be ten years out, to 2021. To do that equation, we can use a Future Value Calculator found on the Internet at http://www.investopedia .com/calculator/FVCal.aspx

We plug in $3.85 as the Present Value; 9.18% for the Interest Rate; and 10 for the number of years; we then hit the calculate button and get a Future Value of $9.27. So if Coca-Cola can continue growing its per share earnings at its historic annual growth rate of 9.18%, we can project that in the year 2021 we will be earning $9.27 a share.

As investment analysts, we can take the projection that Coca-Cola is going to be earning $9.27 a share in 2021 and multiply it by a projected price-to-earnings ratio to come up with a projected market price for Coca-Cola's stock in 2021. Picking the P/E ratio is a serious matter—if we choose a bull market P/E, we could end up with a projection that is insanely high. So what we do is take a look at Coca-Cola's historic average annual P/E ratios for the last ten years and choose the lowest—which will give us a far more conservative valuation.

It is better to be surprised on the upside than have a rude awakening on the down side—which is what can happen if we use a historically high P/E ratio. For the purposes of this book, the P/E ratio we will use for calculating all future valuations will be the lowest for the period between 2001 and 2011.

In looking at the historic P/E ratios for Coca-Cola, we see that they run all the way from a high of 30 in 2001 to a low of 16 in 2009. In 2011 Coca-Cola, with its stock trading at $65 a share, has a P/E of 16.88. But being the conservative analysts that we are, we will use 16 for calculating Coca-Cola's 2021 future per share earnings.

If we take Coca-Cola's projected 2021 per share earnings of $9.27 and multiply it by 16, we get a projected market price of $148.32 a share.

Now we can calculate a projected annual rate of return on our 2011 $65 a share investment by going back to our Rate of Return Calculator, http://www.moneychimp.com/calculator/discount_rate_calculator.htm

We plug in $65 a share for the Present Value, which is what we paid for the stock in 2011; we then punch in our projected 2021 stock price of $148.32 a share for the Future Value; add 10 for the Number of Years; and hit the "compute" button to get a projected annual rate of return of 8.60% for the ten-year period.

Present Value = $65

Future Value = $148.32

Number of Years = 10

Projected Annual Rate of Return = 8.6%

The question then becomes, do you find an annual rate of return of 8.6% attractive?

DIVIDEND COMPONENT

With Coca-Cola, we have a dividend component that can be added to our calculation of future value. Coca-Cola has raised its dividend every year for the last ten years. If it can just maintain its 2011 dividend of $1.88 a share till 2021, we can add in $18.80 to our 2021 projected share value of $148.32, boosting our 2021 valuation up to $167.12, which increases our annual rate of return for the ten-year period to 9.9%.

WORD OF WARNING

We have to add one BIG WARNING: This kind future earnings projection works only with companies with a durable competitive advantage and a history of consistent and stable earnings. And it should only be done using historically low P/E ratios. (Trying to use this kind of long-term earnings projection with a company that has an erratic profit history—like Ford Motor or United Continental—can be very dangerous to the health of your portfolio.)

CHAPTER 6

Using Per Share Book Value History to Help Identify a Company with a Consumer Monopoly

Book value has long had a place in Grahamian value investing; it is calculated by going to the company's balance sheet and finding the equity value, then dividing that by the number of shares outstanding. The company's equity value is calculated by subtracting the company's liabilities from its assets, with the difference being its equity value. If you take $100 million in assets, less $90 million in liabilities, you get $10 million in equity. If the company has $10 million in equity and one million shares outstanding, it would have a book value of $10 a share ($10 million ÷ 1 million shares = $10). To make it easier, whenever you see "book value" just think per share book value. Basically, book value is the per share equity value of the company.

Warren likes to point out that there is a difference between "tangible book value" and "book value." With the calculation of "per share book value," assets include such intangibles as goodwill; but in the calculation of "per share tangible book value," intangibles are not included in the calculation of assets, which lowers the amount of assets a company has, and thus its tangible book value. Why is this important? In the old days Warren made his living buying companies that were selling for less than their tangible book value. But here we are interested in using the long-term growth of book value as a way of quickly identifying a company with a durable competitive advantage; as such, we should rely on the historical per share "book value" provided by investment services such as Value Line Investment Survey. (Note: Warren has used Value Line as a source for financial information for over fifty years.)

With Warren's own Berkshire Hathaway, he has used the growth of Berkshire's book value as a method for measuring Berkshire's long-term economic performance. This is not the same as using book value as a measure of the intrinsic value of a company—its book value is $40 a share; therefore, the company's intrinsic value is $40 a share. The intrinsic value of a business is its future income stream discounted to present value—which is a near-impossible calculation to make with any accuracy. But it is safe to say that on any given day, the per share intrinsic value of a company may be much more or a lot less than its book value. The two seldom match up perfectly.

Most companies with a durable competitive advantage

have a per share intrinsic value that is far in excess of what its book value is. However, there are a few companies that have a durable competitive advantage and a negative book value— like Moody's—but these kinds of businesses are few and far between. If you see a long-term upward trend in per share earnings and a negative book value, it is a safe assumption that you are dealing with a company that has some kind of durable competitive advantage working in its favor.

Here we are using growth in book value to help us measure growth in the company's underlying intrinsic value. A method that Warren endorses is:

> We give you Berkshire's book-value figures because they today serve as a rough, albeit significantly understated, tracking measure for Berkshire's intrinsic value. In other words, the percentage change in book value in any given year is likely to be reasonably close to that year's change in intrinsic value.

Long-term growth in book value can be used as a loose method for measuring long-term growth in the intrinsic value of a business. It can also be used in helping us identify companies with a durable competitive advantage. One of the first things that we look at when searching for a company with a durable competitive advantage is whether or not its book value is growing over time.

Let's compare Coca-Cola to Ford Motor Company.

From 1995 to 2011 Coca-Cola showed a 579% increase in per share book value—growing at a compounding annual rate of 12.72% for the last sixteen years. Over the last ten years, its per share book value has grown 219%, at an annual compounding rate of 12.32%.

YEAR	BVPS (Book Value Per Share, $)
'11	14.60
'10	13.43
'09	10.77
'08	8.85
'07	9.38
'06	7.30
'05	6.90
'04	6.61
'03	5.77
'02	4.78
'01	4.57
'00	3.75
'99	3.85
'98	3.41
'97	2.96
'96	2.48
'95	2.15

From 1995 to 2011 Ford Motor showed a -86.48% decline in book value—decreasing at a compounding annual rate of -11.76% for the last sixteen years. Over the last ten years, its per share book value has decreased -32%, at an annual compounding rate of -3.82%.

YEAR	BVPS (Book Value Per Share, $)
'11	2.90
'10	0.40
'09	-2.43
'08	- 7.22
'07	2.55
'06	-1.83
'05	7.02
'04	8.76
'03	6.36
'02	3.07
'01	4.28
'00	9.75
'99	22.53
'98	20.36
'97	24.83
'96	21.91
'95	21.45

It's pretty clear that from a long-term investment perspective, Coca-Cola is a business that is growing its intrinsic value, while Ford Motor is a company that has a shrinking intrinsic value.

This test is far from perfect—there are lots of reasons that a company's book value might shrink that have nothing to do with the underlying economics of the business. A company could spin off a subsidiary company to its shareholder, which would decrease the parent company's book value.

And there are lots of reasons why a company's book value might increase that really don't have anything to do with an increase in the company's intrinsic value—like buying another company at an insanely lofty price, which jacks up the value that is placed on the books of the acquiring company. But those issues really don't concern us, because here we are using long-term growth of book value as a loose indicator of the presence of a durable competitive advantage, which is our main concern. Once we think we've identified its presence, we then can delve deeper into the company's economic history to help us determine whether a durable competitive advantage is truly present. Now let's take a look at the companies in Buffett's stock portfolio.

THE
CASE STUDIES
AND VALUATIONS

CHAPTER 7

American Express Company

Address:
200 Vesey Street
New York, NY 10285 USA
Telephone: (212) 640-2000
Website: www.americanexpress.com

Industry: Global Payments, Charge and Credit Cards, Travel
Service

Key Statistics:
Public Company
Founded in 1850
Employees: 58,300
Revenue: $30.2 billion (2011)
Net Earnings: $4.85 billion (2011)
Per Share Earnings: $4.05 (2011)
Ten-Year Average Annual Growth for Per Share Earnings:
12.2%
Per Share Book Value: $16.60 (2011)
Market Price: $45 a share (2011)
Dividend/Yield 2011: $0.72/1.37%
Years of Berkshire Purchase: 1994, 1995, 1998, 2000
Average Per Share Price Berkshire Paid: $8.44
Stock Exchanges: NYSE
Ticker Symbol: AXP

As of 2011, Berkshire owns 151,610,700 shares, or 12.6%, of American Express's outstanding shares, which it purchased in the period from 1994 to 2000. With American Express trading at $45 a share in 2011, Berkshire's position is worth approximately $6.82 billion; with a total cost $1.28 billion, Berkshire has a gain of $5.54 billion on this investment.

American Express is a worldwide financial services company headquartered in New York City, is one of 30 companies that make up the Dow Jones Industrial Average, and is ranked by *Businessweek* and Interbrand as the twenty-second most valuable brand in the world. Its Amex Cards have 24% of the credit card transactions in the United States, the most of any single card issuer.

Started in 1850 by Henry Wells and William Fargo, the same men who founded Wells Fargo Bank, American Express was originally a mail transport company. With the westward expansion of the country and the discovery of gold in California, it jumped into the mail-order money business in 1882 as a way to profit from a new nation's need to quickly ship money back and forth between the east and west coasts.

When C. J. Fargo (William's younger brother) went to Europe in 1888 he became frustrated at how difficult it was to get cash using traditional letters of credit, so when he returned to the States, he came up with the idea of the

American Express travelers checks, which required it to set up offices and banking relationships all over the world. The traveler's check business also gave American Express "float" to invest—you paid for the checks but often didn't spend the money for two or more months. American Express got free use of your money until you spent it. American Express promptly invested cash in short-term commercial debt sold to it by none other than Goldman Sachs. This "free use of the float" was one of the reasons that the traveler's check business was so profitable.

The American Express card was introduced to U.S. customers in 1957 following the success of the rival Diners Club card, and was offered worldwide in the early 1960s. The card allows the company to earn a fee from the merchant on every customer purchase made with the card. Think of it as a kind of convenience/benefit tax that the customer and merchant have to pay. Consumers pay a flat annual fee for the convenience of not having to carry cash and receiving a monthly summary for the accountant along with a nice, healthy rewards program to keep them using the card. The merchant pays 2.5% of the sale for the benefit of having a customer who walks in the door with a large amount of credit to spend—via the card—and the comfort of knowing that the check won't bounce. Until the American Express card was introduced, using a check was about the only way to make a really big purchase unless you carried cash.

So what competitive advantage does American Express have over its competition? When you use your American Express Card the company makes more money per transaction than does MasterCard or Visa. With MasterCard and Visa there is an Issuing Bank, which issues the card to the customer; and there is the Acquiring Bank, which processes the transaction for the merchant where the customer used the card. There is also the Network (MasterCard and Visa), which acts as a link between the Issuing Bank and the Acquiring Bank. On average the merchant is charged a fee of 1.9% of the entire sale—0.1% of this goes to the acquiring bank and 1.7% to the issuing bank, while the network gets 0.09%. Most of what the Issuing Bank earns goes to rewards programs and cash back. Real money is made by the credit card company on the interest it charges its customers when they don't get the card paid off in time.

American Express is different in that it acts as all three: the Issuing Bank, the Acquiring Bank, and the Network. The company keeps the entire fee, and the fee it keeps is 2.5% of the merchant's sale. This is a much nicer place to be. And since the American Express Card is generally issued to higher-net-worth individuals and corporations, the default rate on payment is much lower than it is with the credit card issuers who issue cards to the middle class.

American Express is one of those "Buffett" businesses that actually benefits over time from inflation. As inflation causes prices to rise, the amount the customer has to pay the merchant increases, and since the merchant pays 2.5% of the sales price to American Express, as inflation lifts prices, American Express earns more money. Consider this: $100 million in merchant sales in 1975, because of inflation, would equate to $400 million in merchant sales in 2011. (One of the reasons we have inflation is that our government likes to print money.) In 1975 American Express would have earned a fee of $2.5 million on the $100 million in sales ($100 million x .025 = $2.5 million), but in 2011 it would have earned a fee of $10 million on the $400 million in sales ($400 million x .025 = $10 million). The same quantity of goods traded hands in 2011 as in 1975. However, inflation made it cost more, and in the process of the higher cost, American Express made more money.

The economic history of American Express proves Buffett's transaction inflation theory. In 1994 American Express had revenue of $14 billion, and in 2011 it had revenue of $29 billion, which equates to an average annual increase in revenue of 4.8%. We can argue that out of that rise in revenue, 2.4% of it was due to inflation over that period—in other words, half the growth in American Express's revenue can be attributed to the effects of inflation. Inflation allows American Express to make more and more money over time without additional incremental capital outlays to infrastructure costs.

Warren first got interested in American Express in 1963 during the great Salad Oil Scandal. This had occurred when American Express loaned money against what turned out to be nonexistent collateral: salad oil stored in giant tanks. When American Express went to foreclose on the collateral, the salad oil wasn't there. The ensuing losses—about $80 million—sucked out most of American Express's net worth, driving its stock price down from $80 a share to $30 a share. Warren realized that even if the company lost all of its net worth, its franchises of travelers checks and charge cards were still golden and would keep on earning. So he invested 40% of his partnership's money, $13 million, and in the three short years following the debacle, he sold off his position at a profit of nearly $20 million.

Warren reasoned that American Express's salad oil loss was no different than if the company had paid out a dividend to its shareholders that had taken most of its net worth. This is something a company with a durable competitive advantage can do because it is a business that year after year generates more money than it can possibly use in the day-today operations of the business. It doesn't need a large surplus of net worth to keep the money flowing in.

The lesson here is that in a situation where a company with a durable competitive advantage, like American Express, experiences a onetime loss, even a severe one, which decimates the company's stock, the underlying value of its durable competitive advantage will return the company to profitability in short order and, with it, an upward revaluation of the company's stock.

New Buying Opportunity in the Early 1990s

In the early 1990s American Express started losing big money in its brokerage operation, Shearson Lehman Brothers. In 1991, American Express became desperate for additional capital and cut a deal with Warren's Berkshire Hathaway to sell BRK $300 million in convertible preferred stock. (Convertible preferred stock is preferred stock that is convertible into the company's common stock.) What Warren saw was that a division of American Express—Shearson Lehman Brothers— was causing all the problems while the underlying traveler's check and AmEx Card businesses were both still very strong franchises. Warren has often said that a lot of money can be made investing in a company that has a solvable problem— the solution here was right around the corner.

Then, in 1993, after American Express's Shearson unit reported a loss of $116 million, Warren started adding to his position, on the calculation that if American Express got rid of Shearson, the underlying traveler's check and charge card businesses would be able to shine through and lift the price of the stock. And in late 1993 American Express did solve its problem by selling off Shearson for $1 billion.

Warren held on to this position, adding to it in 1994, 1995, 1998, and 2000, growing his American Express holdings to 151,619,700 shares, or 12.6% of the entire company.

AMERICAN EXPRESS'S
PER SHARE EARNINGS HISTORY

American Express's per share earnings history and the growth of its book value present us with a particular challenge because in 2005 the company spun off American Express Financial Advisors to its shareholders, which caused a decrease in its earnings by about $0.24 a share that same year.

Even with American Express Financial Advisors being spun off, we can see that from 2001 to 2011 American Express showed a 216% increase in earnings per share—growing at a compounding annual rate of 12.2% for the last ten years, which included the 2009 banking crisis.

Year	EPS (Earnings Per Share, $)
'11	4.05
'10	3.35
'09	1.54
'08	2.33
'07	3.29
'06	2.82
'05	2.30
'04	2.74
'03	2.31
'02	2.01
'01	1.28

With per share earnings in 2011 at $4.05 and an asking price of $45 a share, we can argue that we are earning an after–corporate tax initial rate of return of $4.05, or 9%; and with that 9% initial rate of return, we can project that per share earnings will increase at their historic annual growth rate of 12.2% ($4.05 ÷ $45 = 9%).

If we can buy American Express at a cheaper price, the "Purchase Price Economics" will improve. In short, a price of $30 a share will mean that our initial after–corporate tax return will increase to 13.5% ($4.05 ÷ $30 = 13.5%). Likewise, if the price of the stock goes up, the Purchase Price Economics will decline: A price of $60 a share will mean an initial after–corporate tax return of 6.7% ($4.05 ÷ $60 = 6.7%). This is one of the reasons that a bear market over the short term always makes Warren smile: The lower price greatly improves the economics of the purchase.

PER SHARE BOOK VALUE HISTORY

American Express's spinoff of American Express Financial Advisors in 2005 alters the picture of its per share book value history by removing approximately $3.80 in book value from the American Express parent. To get a more accurate picture of the growth of its per share book value, we divide it into two periods, 2001 to 2004 and 2005 to 2011. From 2001 to 2004, it grew its per share book value at an annual rate of 10.84%; and from 2005 to 2011 it grew its per share book value at an annual rate of 11.8%.

YEAR	BVPS (Book Value Per Share, $)
'11	16.60
'10	13.55
'09	12.09
'08	10.21
'07	9.52
'06	8.77
'05	8.50
'04	12.31
'03	11.93
'02	10.62
'01	9.04

In 2011 American Express had a per share book value of approximately $16.60 a share and was earning approximately $4.05 a share. We can argue that as an equity bond, it's earning an annual after–corporate tax rate of return of 24% ($4.05 ÷ $16.60 = 24%).

But we can't buy it at its per share book value of $16.60; we have to pay the stock market price in 2011 of approximately $45 a share. This means we can argue that we are going to be earning an after–corporate tax initial rate of return on our American Express equity bond of 9% ($4.05 ÷ $45 = 9%). The after–corporate tax initial rate of return will increase as the company increases its earnings, which we are projecting will remain at the company's historic annual growth rate of 12.2%.

The next question is what will a $4.05 initial rate of return growing at an annual rate of approximately 12.2% look like in ten years? To help us determine this future value, we need to use the Future Value Calculator located on the Internet at http://www.investopedia.com/calculator/FVCal.aspx

First, plug in: 12.2% for the Interest Rate Per Time Period; $4.05 for the Present Value; and 10 for the number of Time Periods; then click the calculate button to get $12.81. This means that if we pay $45 for a share of American Express stock in 2011, by 2021 it will be earning $12.81 a share, which equates to an after–corporate tax return of 28.4% on our $45-a-share investment.

Now what will that $12.81, or 28.4%, return be worth to us in 2021? That all depends on what price-to-earnings ratio the stock market is valuing the stock at in 2012. In the case of American Express, over the last ten years it has had P/E ratios that ranged from 30.2 to 12.4. Since Warren likes to play out his analysis from a conservative perspective, we will use the P/E ratio of 12.4. With a projected P/E of 12.4, we can project that the stock will be trading at $158.84 a share in 2021. If we bought American Express stock at $45 a share in 2011 and sold it for $158.84 a share in 2021, our total gain of the sale would be $113.84 a share, giving us a total return of 252% and an annual rate of return of 13.4% for the ten-year period.

Though American Express has raised its dividend every year for the last 10 years, if it can just maintain its 2011 dividend of $0.72 a share until 2021, we can add in $7.20 to our $158.84 sale proceeds, boosting our total proceeds from sale and dividends up to $166.04, which increases our total return to 268% and our annual rate of return to 13.95% for the ten-year period.

The question now is does a potential ten-year annual rate of return of 13.95% interest you? For Warren it is interesting enough to keep his $6.82 billion worth of American Express stock on Berkshire's books.

CHAPTER 8

The Bank of New York Mellon (BNY Mellon)

Address:
One Wall Street
New York, NY 10286 USA
Telephone: (212) 495-1784
Website: http://www.bnymellon.com

Industry: Banking/Financial Services

Key Statistics:
Public Company
Founded in 1784
Employees: 42,200
Net Earnings: $2.98 billion (2011)
Per Share Earnings: $2.40 (2011)
Ten-Year Average Annual Growth for Per Share Earnings:
  2.86%
Per Share Book Value: $28.00
Ten-Year Average Annual Growth for Per Share Book Value:
  12.45%
Current Market Price: $21 a share
Dividend/Yield 2011: $0.52/2.4%
Year of Berkshire Purchase: 2010
Average Per Share Price Berkshire Paid: $26
Stock Exchanges: NYSE
Ticker Symbol: BK

This is a new investment for Berkshire and was acquired in the 2010/2011 period. As of the middle of 2011, Berkshire owns 1,992,759 shares, or less than 1% of BNY Mellon's outstanding shares. With BNY Mellon trading at $21 a share, Berkshire's position is worth approximately $41.8 million; with a cost of approximately $51 million, Berkshire has a $9.15 million loss on this investment due to declines in the stock market—which, from Buffett's perspective, makes it an even better long-term investment because of the underlying long-term business economics of the company.

When it comes to financial companies, Warren likes old, and the older the better. BNY Mellon was formed in 2007 by the merger of The Bank of New York, the oldest bank in the United States, formed in 1784 by founding father Alexander Hamilton, and Mellon Financial Corporation, which was one of the world's largest money management firms. The combined entity, BNY Mellon, is a global financial service company with more than 40,000 staff and has more than $1.2 trillion under management. It is in the top 10 global wealth managers. It is also the world's leading asset servicer, with $25 trillion in assets under custody or administration. It services more than $11 trillion in debt for its corporate clients—BNY Mellon is the one sending out the checks to the individual bondholders. It primarily operates in the fields of asset management, asset service, wealth management, and broker-dealer and advisory services. It is the largest securities-servicing and asset-management firm in the world, with oper-ations in thirty-seven different countries, servicing a hundred different markets.

BNY Mellon is not a retail lender like Wells Fargo or Bank of America. It is a kind of bank that services other corporations and financial institutions and manages money for investors via subsidiaries such as Dreyfus—which manages investors' wealth through hundreds of mutual funds and investment trusts under its control.

BNY Mellon suffered a setback in 2008 and 2009, having invested in mortgage-backed securities, which decimated its earnings in 2009 as it wrote off its losses. But in 2011 it is set to report record earnings. It was hired by the U.S. Treasury for $20 million to act as the master custodian for the TARP funds, handling accounting and record keeping for the program.

The durable competitive advantage BNY Mellon has is its size, lower costs, and expertise. No one is bigger or cheaper or does it better. Here, economics of scale comes into play, making it the best game in town. One of the keys to its success and what makes it "different" from other banks is that it is in the business, managing money and providing services to institutional money managers; that mutual fund that you have invested money in more than likely banks with BNY Mellon. When you go to sell some of your shares in a mutual fund, it is BNY Mellon that handles the transaction. And that

Exchange Traded Fund that owns that basket of securities that you own shares in, holds that basket of securities through BNY Mellon. On top of that, BNY Mellon has a massive worldwide money management operation that services pension funds, corporations, foundations, and individual investors. Needless to say, it is not your normal bank.

How about all those troubled loans that have been haunting the banking industry? In 2011 BNY Mellon registered approximately $30 million in Loan Loss Provisions against approximately $3.2 billion in net income. Which gives it a considerable margin of safety. (Consider this: In 2011 Wells Fargo had approximately $14 billion in Loan Loss Provisions against an after-tax net income of $15 billion. A comfortable cushion, but nowhere close to what BNY Mellon has going on.)

Note: Since BNY Mellon is the result of a merger in 2007, our historic numbers are the result of a consolidation of the two companies' financials for the last ten years.

What Warren Finds Interesting

Let's start with the obvious: In 2011 BNY Mellon is trading under or near its book value. Which means that you can buy at or below its per share equity value. And, since the combined banks historically have consistently shown a better-than-10% return on shareholders' equity—some years over 20%—Warren can argue that he is getting an equity bond at its book value that will be delivering an annual return in the neighborhood of 10% to 20%.

In fact, in 2011 it will earn approximately $2.40 a share— which, if we buy it at $21 a share, will give us an initial after–corporate tax rate of return of 11.4%.

If we look at BNY Mellon's per share earnings history, we can see that from 2001 to 2011 it showed a 32.6% increase in earnings per share—with a single losing year in 2009—but overall, growth at a compounding annual rate of 2.86% for the last ten years.

Year	EPS (Earnings Per Share, $)
'11	2.40
'10	2.14
'09	(1.07)
'08	1.20
'07	2.18
'06	1.93
'05	2.03
'04	1.85
'03	1.52
'02	1.24
'01	1.81

With per share earnings in 2011 at $2.40, and an asking price of $21 a share, we can argue that we are earning an after–corporate tax initial rate of return of $2.40, or 11.4%; and we can predict that that 12.1% initial rate of return will grow at an annual rate of 2.86%.

PER SHARE BOOK VALUE HISTORY

From 2001 to 2011 BNY Mellon showed a 223% increase in per share book value—never having a losing year and growing at a compounding annual rate of 12.45% for the last ten years. Which is not too shabby. Remember, we want to see the underlying value of the business increasing over time; it's a good sign that the business is benefiting from some kind of long-term durable competitive advantage.

YEAR	BVPS (Book Value Per Share, $)
'11	28.00
'10	26.63
'09	23.97
'08	22.00
'07	25.66
'06	15.34
'05	12.81
'04	11.93
'03	10.87
'02	9.21
'01	8.66

In 2011 BNY Mellon had a per share book value of $28.00 and was earning approximately $2.40 a share. We can argue that as an equity bond, it is earning an annual rate of return of 8.57%. In this rare case, in 2011, we can actually buy BNY Mellon below its per share book value, $28.00. If we pay the 2011 stock market price of approximately $21 a share, we can project that we are going to be earning an after–corporate tax initial rate of return on our BNY Mellon equity bond of 11.4% ($2.40 ÷ $21 = 11.4%), and that this initial after–corporate tax rate of return, 11.4%, will increase as the company increases its earnings, which we are projecting will be at their historic annual per share growth rate of 2.86%.

The next question is what will a $2.40 initial after–corporate tax rate of return growing at an annual rate of approximately 2.86% look like in ten years? To help us determine this future value, we need to use the Future Value Calculator located on the Internet at http://www.investopedia.com/calculator/FVCal.aspx

Plug in: 2.86% for the Interest Rate Per Time Period; $2.40 for the Present Value; and 10 for the number of Time Periods; then click the calculate button and get $3.18. Which means that if we pay $21 for a share of BNY Mellon stock, by 2021 it will be earning $3.18 a share, which equates to an after–corporate tax return of 15.14% on our $21-a-share investment.

Now what will that $3.18, or 15.14%, be worth to us in 2021? That all depends on what price-to-earnings ratio the stock market is valuing the stock at in 2021. If it is at its 2011 P/E ratio of 12 (which is its ten-year low), then we can project that the stock will be trading at $38.16 a share.

If we bought our BNY Mellon stock at $21 a share in 2011 and sold it for $38.16 a share in 2021, our total gain from the sale would be $17.16 a share, giving us a total return of 81.71% and an annual rate of return of 6.15% for the ten-year period.

Though BNY Mellon dropped its dividend in the financial debacle of 2009, in 2011 it is paying a dividend of $0.52 a share. If it can just maintain its 2011 dividend of $0.52 a share until 2021, we can add in $5.20 to our $38.16 gross proceeds from the sale, boosting our proceeds from sale and dividends up to $43.36. This bumps up our total return to 106% and our annual rate of return to 7.52%.

The question now is, does a potential ten-year annual rate of return of 7.52% interest you? Warren found it interesting enough to invest $51 million in the company over the last twenty-four months.

CHAPTER 9

Coca-Cola Company

Address:
One Coca-Cola Plaza
Atlanta, Georgia 30313 USA
Telephone: (404) 676-2121
Website: http://www.coca-cola.com

Industry: Beverage
Area Served: Worldwide

Key Statistics:
Public Company
Founded in 1886
Employees: 139,800
Sales: $46.2 billion (2011)
Net Earnings: $8.76 billion (2011)
Per Share Earnings: $3.85 (2011)
Average Annual Growth for Per Share Earnings: 9.18%
Per Share Book Value: $14.60
Average Annual Growth for Per Share Book Value: 12.32%
Dividend/Yield 2011: $1.88/2.8%
Years of Berkshire Purchase: 1988, 1989, 1994
Average Per Share Price Berkshire Paid: $6.50
Stock Exchanges: NYSE
Ticker Symbol: KO

As of 2011 Berkshire owns 200 million shares, or 8.6% of Coca-Cola's outstanding common stock, at a cost of $1.299 billion. With Coca-Cola trading at $65 a share, Berkshire's position is worth approximately $13 billion.

Coca-Cola is the one product that took over the world.

Coca-Cola was invented in 1886 by John Pemberton, a pharmacist who owned the Pemberton Chemical Company in Atlanta. A Confederate veteran, Pemberton was severely wounded in the American Civil War. During treatment for his injury, he became addicted to morphine. He tried to find a cure for his addiction and started experimenting with a coca wine concoction called Vin Mariani, which was made from kola, coca, and damiana (a South American aphrodisiac). He worked with another Atlanta pharmacist named Willis Venable to perfect his new remedy—which was eventually named Coca-Cola for its two main ingredients. Coca-Cola was first sold in 1886 at Jacobs Pharmacy in Atlanta, and sold only 25 gallons the first year. Four years later, Pemberton sold the formula to Asa Candler, a drugstore entrepreneur and promoter extraordinaire, who paid $2,300 (about $55,000 in today's dollars) to Pemberton and a few other shareholders for the rights to what eventually became the best-selling beverage in the world.

One of the first moves that Candler made was to focus

on selling just the syrup concentrate to soda fountains across the nation. He intentionally stayed away from the capital-intensive bottling business, which required major investments in plant and equipment, and instead set up Coca-Cola syrup manufacturing plants around the U.S. to make Coca-Cola readily available to his customers. This "syrup business model" allowed for a rapid and profitable expansion of the business, and by 1895 Coca-Cola was consumed in every state and territory in the union.

Though several people tried to bottle Coke during this period, Candler wasn't impressed with the end result and tended to discourage bottling. In 1899 two enterprising Chattanooga, Tennessee, lawyers, Benjamin Thomas and Joseph Whitehead, traveled to Atlanta to try to convince Candler to grant them exclusive rights to bottle Coca-Cola for much of America. At first Candler was resistant, but he soon saw what Thomas and Whitehead were talking about. There were already 3,000-plus bottlers of other beverages scattered around America. If Thomas and Whitehead had an exclusive master license, they could go around the country licensing the bottling of Coca-Cola to the different bottlers, and it wouldn't cost Candler a dime. Better still, this strategy had the potential to make him a fortune. This was one of the first franchising schemes in America. It ensured the consistency and quality of the product, and committed the franchisees to buy only

Coca-Cola syrup from the Coca-Cola company—which made Candler very happy.

Candler said yes to the deal. Thomas and Whitehead went back to Chattanooga and started haggling with each other about how best to utilize the exclusive license. Eventually they decided to divide it up geographically. Thomas took the East Coast and Chattanooga, while Whitehead took the South and West. The plan was to grant sublicenses to the different independent bottlers in exchange for a portion of the bottlers' profits. Thomas had an advantage in that the East Coast already had a well-established bottling industry. But Whitehead had a much harder task; while bottling was well established in the South, it was still in its infancy in the West. To help build the business, Whitehead partnered with another Chattanooga lawyer and businessman by the name of John T. Lupton. Together they provided the license and financing for subfranchisees to start, in exchange for half their profits. (Seventy-eight years later, Lupton's grandson sold his family's licensing and bottling license back to Coca-Cola for $1.8 billion.)

By the end of 1918 there were nearly a thousand plants across America bottling Coca-Cola. This was a huge economic success for Candler's syrup business. In 1919 he sold the Coca-Cola Company to Atlanta banker Ernest Woodruff and a group of investors for $25 million. Woodruff and his investors immediately took Coca-Cola public at $40 a share.

While Candler had been obsessed with selling Coca-Cola to the American public, Woodruff would spend the next sixty years selling it to the world.

Woodruff introduced Coca-Cola to the 1928 Olympic Games in Amsterdam. He also pushed the development and promotion of the now-ubiquitous six-pack. Before, Coca-Cola had been sold only as single bottles and by the case. With the advent of electricity and the development of refrigeration, Woodruff oversaw the creation of the Coca-Cola cooler and later the Coca-Cola coin-operated soda machine. By 1940, under Woodruff's direction, Coca-Cola was being bottled and sold in forty-four countries outside the U.S. This was the beginning of Woodruff's world conquest.

During World War II Woodruff said that any serviceman or -woman in uniform would pay only 5 cents for a bottle of Coca-Cola (as opposed to 10 cents) wherever they were, whatever it cost the company. During the war, at the request of Supreme Commander of the Allied Forces General Dwight Eisenhower, Woodruff built sixty-four bottling plants to supply some five billion bottles of Coke consumed by servicemen and -women during the war. This set the stage for even greater international expansion after the war. In many countries Coca-Cola was the only bottled beverage available.

In the 1950s and the 1960s the company decided to take advantage of its distribution network and branch out into other flavors: Fanta, Tab, and Fresca were introduced. In 1960 Coca-Cola acquired the Minute Maid Company, which broadened its market penetration and gave it new avenues to explore, such as the breakfast orange juice market.

During the 1970s and 1980s, the bottling industry, which was made up of many individual bottling companies all over the world, began to consolidate. Coca-Cola helped facilitate the consolidation by investing in the new bottling entities. This ensured that the company's largest international partners would have the means to service the growing global demand. In 1981 Robert C. Goizueta became chairman and CEO of the Coca-Cola Company. One of the first things he did was to spearhead the consolidation of the American bottling companies into a new public company called Coca-Cola Enterprises. He also introduced Diet Coke, which in two years became the world's best-selling diet soda and the most popular soda after Coca-Cola.

During the stock market crash of 1987, Warren started making his first investments in Coca-Cola; by the end of 1989 Berkshire had acquired $1.023 billion of the stock. He'd add to his position again in 1994, taking it to 200 million shares (adjusted for splits), bringing his total cost up to $1.299 billion. In 2011 he still has the same 200 million shares and they have grown to be worth $13 billion.

In the 1990s the company expanded its line of beverages

to include the sport drink Powerade, the children's fruit drink Qoo, and the bottled water Dasani. It also acquired the Cadbury Schweppes beverage brands in more that 120 different countries. Today, Coca-Cola markets more than 100 different beverage products in more than 200 countries throughout the world, and sells more than 1.6 billion servings of its products every day.

What can we learn from this company's brief history? The same product has created an immense amount of wealth over a very long period of time and it will probably continue to do so for a long, long time to come. Our great-grandchildren will be drinking Coke or one of its many sister beverages. Think predictable product, predictable profits, and little or no research and development costs. This is Warren's kind of business in spades.

Now let's look at some of the numbers and see if things, including our money, really do go better with Coke.

COCA-COLA'S
NET PER SHARE EARNINGS GROWTH

From 2001 to 2011 Coca-Cola showed a 140% increase in its per share earnings, which equates to an annual compounding growth rate of 9.18%.

Year	EPS (Earnings Per Share, $)
'11	3.85
'10	3.49
'09	2.93
'08	3.02
'07	2.57
'06	2.37
'05	2.17
'04	2.06
'03	1.95
'02	1.65
'01	1.60

With per share earnings in 2011 of $3.85 and an asking price of $65 a share, we can project that we are earning an after–corporate tax initial rate of return of $3.85 or 5.9%; we also can project that that 5.9% initial rate of return will grow at an annual rate of approximately 9.18%.

Per Share Book Value History

From 2001 to 2011 Coca-Cola showed a 219% increase in per share book value—never having a losing year and growing at a compounding annual rate of 12.32% for the last ten years, which is exactly what Warren is looking for, a company with an increasing underlying value that grows year after year.

Year	BVPS (Book Value Per Share, $)
'11	14.60
'10	13.53
'09	10.77
'08	8.85
'07	9.38
'06	7.30
'05	6.90
'04	6.61
'03	5.77
'02	4.78
'01	4.57

BUFFETT BUY ANALYSIS

In 2011 Coca-Cola had a per share book value of $14.60 and was earning approximately $3.85 a share. This means we can argue that as an equity bond, it is earning an annual rate of return of 26.3% ($3.85 ÷ $14.60 = 26.3%).

Since we can't buy it at its per share book value of $14.60, we have to pay the stock market price in 2011 of approximately $65 a share; this means we can argue that we are going to be earning an after–corporate tax initial rate of return on our Coca-Cola equity bond of 5.9% ($3.85 ÷ $65 = 5.9%), but that after–corporate tax initial rate of return will increase as the company increases its earnings, which we are projecting will be at their historic per share annual growth rate of 9.18%.

The next question is what will a $3.85 initial after–corporate rate of return growing at an annual rate of approximately 9.18% look like in ten years? We'll use the Future Value Calculator located on the Internet at http://www.investopedia.com/calculator/FVCal.aspx

Plug in: 9.18% for the Interest Rate Per Time Period; $3.85 for the Present Value; and 10 for the number of Time Periods; then click the calculate button and get $9.27. This means that if we pay $65 for a share of Coca-Cola stock in 2011, by 2021 it will be earning $9.27 a share, which equates to a 14.2% rate of return on our $65-a-share investment ($9.27 ÷ $65 = 14.2%).

Now what will that $9.27, or 14.2%, be worth to us in 2021? If the price-to-earnings ratio that the stock market is valuing the stock at in 2021 is 16 (which is the historic low), then we can project that the stock will be trading at $148.32 a share ($9.27 x 16 = $148.32). If we bought Coca-Cola stock at $65 a share in 2011 and sold it for $148.32 a share in 2021, our total gain from the sale would be $83.32 a share, giving us a total return of 128% and an annual rate of return of 8.6% for the ten-year period.

Coca-Cola has raised its dividend every year for the last ten years. If it can maintain its 2011 dividend of $1.88 a share till 2021, we can add $18.80 to our $148.32 proceeds from the sale, boosting proceeds from sale and dividends combined up to $167.12, which increases our potential total return to 157% and our annual rate of return to 9.9%.

Do you find a potential annual rate of return of 9.9% for ten years interesting? For Warren it is exciting enough for him to invest $13 billion worth of Coca-Cola stock in Berkshire's frig (vault).

CHAPTER 10

ConocoPhillips

Address:
600 North Dairy Ashford
Houston, TX 77079 USA
Telephone: (918) 661-6600
Website: http://www.conocophillips.com

Industry: Global Oil and Petrochemical Company

Key Statistics:
Public Company
Founded in 1877
Employees: 33,800
Sales: $25.1 billion (2011)
Net Earnings: $9.9 billion (2011)
Per Share Earnings: $8.35 (2011)
Average Annual Growth for Per Share Earnings:
    11.15%
Per Share Book Value: $54.20 (2011)
Average Annual Growth for Per Share Book Value:
    11.19%
Dividend/Yield 2011: $2.64/4.17%(2011)
Date of Berkshire Purchase: 2006 to 2007
Average Price Berkshire Paid: $69.66 a share
Stock Exchanges: NYSE
Ticker Symbol: COP

As of 2011 Berkshire owns 29,109,636 shares, or 2% of ConocoPhillips's outstanding shares. With ConocoPhillips stock trading at $67 a share in 2011, Berkshire's position is worth approximately $1.95 billion; with a cost of $2,028 billion or $69.66 a share, Berkshire has a loss of $78 million on this investment. Which is due to the current down stock market—from Warren's perspective the lower price makes it a better long-term investment as long as the company has a durable competitive advantage.

ConocoPhillips is an oil and petrochemical company with operations all over the world. It was created in 2000 by the merger of Conoco Inc. and Phillips Petroleum. It is the third largest U.S. integrated energy company, based on its proven reserves and production of oil and natural gas. It is also the largest refiner in the United States. It sells fuel under the Conoco, Phillips 66, and 76 brands in North America and Jet in Europe.

Both Conoco and Phillips Petroleum have long and colorful histories. Conoco was founded in Ogden, Utah, in 1875 by Isaac Blake, who saw that the residents of Ogden were using candles and whale oil to light their businesses and homes, since kerosene was available but very expensive. Blake figured that with the coming of the railroad he could buy kerosene in bulk from cheap manufacturers back east and then ship it to Ogden by rail, and be able to sell it at a low enough price that it would stimulate demand, which it did. Then Blake cashed in on the California gold rush by shipping kerosene by rail to Los Angeles and then shipping it by boat to San Francisco, where it was packaged and sold to the miners in the gold fields in Northern California. From there the company grew. But it made its biggest advance during World War II as a supplier of airplane fuel to American forces all over the world.

Phillips Petroleum got its start when a couple of wildcatters by the name of Frank and L. E. Phillips went looking for oil in Oklahoma and hit eighty-one gushers in a row. Twelve years later they founded the Phillips Petroleum Company in Bartlesville, Oklahoma. By 1927 it was pumping fifty-five thousand barrels of oil from more than two thousand wells that it owned in Oklahoma and Texas, and it was opening the first of what would grow to be ten thousand service stations.

By 2000 both of the companies had grown into global giants. And in 2002 Phillips Petroleum acquired Conoco, creating the seventh largest holder of proven reserves and the fourth largest refiner in the world of nongovernmental-controlled entities.

One of the most interesting things about ConocoPhillips is that it has approximately 10.3 billion barrels in proven oil reserves, which means that at an $80-a-barrel price for oil in 2011, its proven reserves have a value of $824 billion, which, on a per share basis, equates to $588 a share. The same 10.3 billion barrels of oil would only have been worth $25 a barrel in 2002, which equates to a total worth of $247 billion or $183 a share. From 2002 to 2011 the value of its oil in the ground nearly tripled. When Warren started buying the stock in 2006, oil was at $60 a barrel and ConocoPhillips had 9.4 billion barrels of oil, with a total market value of $563 billion or $343 a share.

Historically Warren has avoided investing in oil and mining companies for the simple reason that when the company was finished pumping out the oil or digging out the gold, all that was left was an empty hole in the ground. But in this case the underlying value of the oil-in-the-ground increased to the point that its per share value was way in excess of the market price for the stock—an asking price of $44 a share versus an oil-in-the-ground value of $343 a share. That is a large margin of safety that predicts this investment has the potential to be very profitable.

BUFFETT BUY ANALYSIS

If we look at ConocoPhillips's per share earnings history, we can see that from 2001 to 2011 it showed a 187% increase in earnings per share and an overall annual compounding growth rate of 11.15% for the last ten years.

Year	EPS (Earnings Per Share, $)
'11	8.35
'10	5.92
'09	3.24
'08	10.66
'07	9.14
'06	9.99
'05	9.35
'04	5.79
'03	3.35
'02	1.56
'01	2.90

With ConocoPhillips's per share earnings in 2011 at $8.35 and with an asking price of $67 a share, we can argue that we are earning an after–corporate tax initial rate of return of $8.35 or 12.4% ($8.35 ÷ $67 = 12.4%); and we can argue that that 12.4% initial rate of return will grow at the historic per share earnings annual growth rate of 11.15%.

PER SHARE BOOK VALUE HISTORY

From 2001 to 2011 ConocoPhillips showed a 188% increase in per share book value—growing at a compounding annual rate of 11.19% for the last ten years.

Year	BVPS (Book Value Per Share, $)
'11	54.20
'10	47.92
'09	42.03
'08	37.27
'07	56.63
'06	50.21
'05	36.22
'04	29.72
'03	25.17
'02	21.59
'01	18.76

In 2011 ConocoPhillips has a per share book value of $54.20 a share and is earning approximately $8.35 a share. That means that we can argue that as an equity bond, it is earning an annual rate of return of 15.4% ($8.35 ÷ $54.20 = 15.4%), which we, as analysts, can project is going to grow at ConocoPhillips's historic per share earnings annual growth rate of 11.15%.

But we can't buy it at its per share book value of $54.20; we have to pay the stock market price in 2011 of approximately $67 a share, which means we will be earning an initial rate of return of 12.46% on per share earnings of $8.35 ($8.35 ÷ $67 = 12.46%).

The next question is what will an $8.35 initial after–corporate tax rate of return growing at an annual rate of 11.15% look like in ten years? To help us determine this future value, we can use the Future Value Calculator located on the Internet at http://www.investopedia.com/calculator/FVCal.aspx

Plug in: 11.15% for the Interest Rate Per Time Period; $8.35 for the Present Value; and 10 for the number of Time Periods; then click the calculate button to get $24.03 a share. Which means that in 2021 we can project that ConocoPhillips will be earning $24.03 a share.

Now what will that $24.03 be worth to us in 2021? That all depends on what price-to-earnings ratio the stock market is valuing ConocoPhillips stock at in 2021. Over the last ten years, ConocoPhillips has had a P/E as high as 17 and as low as 7. If we use the most conservative P/E ratio, which would be 7, we can project that the stock will be trading at $168.21 a share in 2021 ($24.03 x 7 = $168.21). If we bought ConocoPhillips stock at $67 a share in 2011 and sold it for $168.21 a share in 2021, our total gain from the sale would be $101.21 a share, giving us a total return of 151% and an annual rate of return of 9.6% for the ten-year period.

ConocoPhillips has consistently raised its dividend over the last ten years. If it can just maintain its 2011 dividend of $2.64 a share till 2021, we can add in $26.40 to our $168.21 gross proceeds from the sale, boosting our proceeds from sale and dividends up to $194.61, which increases our total return to 190% and our annual rate of return to 11.25%.

Now, as an investor, does a conservative potential annual rate of return of 11.25% for the next ten years perk your interest? For Warren it is interesting enough to keep $1.95 billion worth of ConocoPhillips stock in Berkshire's portfolio.

CHAPTER 11

Costco Wholesale Corporation

Address:
999 Lake Drive
Issaquah, WA 98027 USA
Telephone: (425) 313-8100
Website: http://www.costco.com

Industry: Discount Retail/Food & Wine/Clothing/
Home Furnishings

Key Statistics:
Public Company
Founded in 1983
Employees: 147,000
Sales: $85 billion (2011)
Net Earnings: $1.4 billion (2011)
Per Share Earnings: $3.30 (2011)
Average Annual Growth for Per Share Earnings: 9.85%
Per Share Book Value: $27.90
Average Annual Growth for Per Share Book Value:
9.95%
Dividend/Yield 2011: $0.96/1.1%
Year of Berkshire Purchase: 2002
Average Per Share Price Berkshire Paid: $34
Stock Exchanges: NDQ
Ticker Symbol: COST

As of 2011 Berkshire owns 4,333,363 million shares, or approximately 1% of Costco's outstanding shares. With Costco trading at $81 a share, Berkshire's position is worth approximately $351 million; with a cost of approximately $147 million, Berkshire has a profit of $204 million on this investment.

Costco caters to the upper-middle-class need for high-quality brand-name goods, spirits, and food available in bulk and at bargain prices. Want a good deal on a couple of bottles of Veuve Clicquot champagne? Costco is where you want to shop. Need a dozen high-end Titleist golf balls? Costco's got them too.

Costco is the largest membership chain and the third largest retailer in the United States. It is also the ninth largest retailer in the world and the world's largest merchant of fine wine (which really means "expensive" wine).

Costco got its start in 1983 in Seattle, selling discounted upscale merchandise to the upper middle class and the "want-to-live rich" Microsoft crowd. One of the ways the rich get richer and stay richer is to pay less for the expensive French wine and cheese they consume. Costco facilitates that need in a world-class way, with 416 stores in the U.S., 79 in Canada, 22 in the United Kingdom, 9 in Japan, 7 in Korea, 6 in Taiwan, 1 in Australia, and 32 warehouse stores in Mexico. Costco has gone from zero sales in 1983 to generating $85 billion in sales and $1.4 billion in net profit in 2011.

As Costco gets bigger and bigger, it branches out into selling more and more high-quality brand-name lines of electronics, groceries, golf equipment, car tires, clothing, and cosmetics. It started a travel agency to assist clients to plan their vacations to all those exotic locales that we read about in *The New York Times* travel section. Costco will also sell you prescription drugs. All this is being done with the goal of helping Costco's customers the world over live a richer lifestyle at a discount price.

WHAT WARREN FINDS INTERESTING

Now the first question that Warren asks is, does all this discounting of brand-name products make Costco shareholders any richer? In fact it's the only question that concerns Warren. The quickest way to determine whether a company's shareholders are getting any richer is to check out the long-term trend of the company's per share earnings.

If we look at Costco's per share earnings history, we can see that from 2001 to 2011, over the last ten years, which includes the 2008–2009 banking crisis, its per share earnings have grown 155%, at an annual compounding rate of 9.85%.

Compare Costco's performance to Coca-Cola, the king of durable competitive advantages—whose earnings in the same ten-year period grew 140%, at an annual compounding rate of 9.18%—and it is easy to see why Warren's partner Charlie Munger got so excited about Costco that he joined its board of directors. Costco is a moneymaking retail machine that can run with the best brands in the world.

Year	EPS (Earnings Per Share, $)
'11	3.30
'10	2.93
'09	2.57
'08	2.89
'07	2.63
'06	2.31
'05	2.04
'04	1.86
'03	1.53
'02	1.48
'01	1.29

With per share earnings in 2011 at $3.30 and an asking price of $81 a share, we can argue that we are earning an after–corporate tax initial rate of return of $3.30 or 4.07%; and we can predict that that 4.07% initial rate of return will grow at an annual rate of 9.85%.

From 2001 to 2011 Costco showed a 158% increase in per share book value—growing at a compounding annual rate of 9.95% for the last ten years.

Year	BVPS (Book Value Per Share, $)
'11	27.90
'10	24.98
'09	22.98
'08	21.25
'07	19.73
'06	19.78
'05	18.80
'04	16.48
'03	14.33
'02	12.51
'01	10.81

Along with the rise in per share earnings, Costco has also been able to produce rapid growth in its per share book value. In the race for rapid growth for per share earnings and book value, Costco is one of the leaders of Warren's pack.

Costco as an Investment Today

In 2011 Costco had a per share book value of $27.90 and was earning approximately $3.30 a share. Which means that as an equity bond, it is earning an annual rate of return of 11.82%. But we can't buy Costco at its per share book value of $27.90; we have to pay the stock market price in 2011 of approximately $81 a share, which means we can argue that we are going to be earning an after–corporate tax initial rate of return on our Costco equity bond of 4% ($3.30 ÷ $81 = 4%). That initial after–corporate tax rate of return will increase as the company increases its earnings, which we are projecting will be at its historic per share annual rate of 9.85% as sales and memberships continue to expand.

The next question is what will a $3.30 after–corporate tax rate of return growing at an annual rate of approximately 9.85% look like in ten years? We can use the Future Value Calculator located on the Internet at http://www.investopedia.com/calculator/FVCal.aspx

Plug in: 9.58% for the Interest Rate Per Time Period; $3.30 for the Present Value; and 10 for the number of Time Periods; then click the calculate button and get $8.24. Which means that if we pay $81 for a share of Costco stock in 2011, by 2021 it will be earning $8.24 a share.

Now what will that $8.24 a share be worth to us in 2021? That all depends on what price-to-earnings ratio the stock market is valuing the stock at in 2021. Using the ten-year low P/E of 19.5, we can calculate that the stock will be trading at $160.68 a share ($8.24 x 19.5 = $160.68). If we bought Costco stock at $81 a share in 2011 and sold it for $160.68 a share in 2021, our total gain on the sale would be $79.68 a share, giving us a total return of 98% and an annual rate of return of 7.09% for the ten-year period.

Though Costco didn't start paying a dividend until 2004,

since then it has been consistent in raising it every year for the last seven years. If it can just maintain its 2011 dividend of $0.96 a share till 2021, we can add in $9.60 to our $160.68 gross proceeds from the sale, boosting our proceeds from sale and dividends up to $170.28. The inclusion of the dividends increases our total return to 110% and our annual rate of return to 7.71%.

To run the rate of return equation go to http://www.moneychimp.com/calculator/discount_rate_calculator.htm

Put in $81 for the Present Value; $170.28 for the Future Value; 10 for the Number of Years; and then click the calculate button to get the Compounding Annual Growth Rate, which in this case equals 7.71%.

The question now is, does a potential compounding annual rate of return of 7.71% for ten years interest you? For Warren it is interesting enough to keep $351 million of his money tied up in Costco stock.

CHAPTER 12

GlaxoSmithKline

Address:
UK Address
Glaxo Wellcome House
Berkeley Avenue
Greenford, Middlesex, England

U.S. Office
1 Franklin Plaza
PO Box 7929
Philadelphia, PA 19101 USA
U.S. Telephone: (215) 751-4638
Website: http://www.gsk.com

Industry: Pharmaceutical/Consumer Health Care

Key Statistics:
Public Company
Founded in 1880/1904/1834/1865
Employees: 90,000
Sales: $43 billion (2011)
Net Earnings: $8.7 billion (2011)
Per Share Earnings: $3.80 (2011)
Average Annual Growth for Per Share Earnings: 10.19%
Per Share Book Value: $6.20
Average Annual Growth for Per Share Book Value: 5.62%

Dividend/Yield 2011: $2.08/5.3%
Year of Berkshire Purchase: 2007
Average Per Share Price Berkshire Paid: $50
Stock Exchanges: NYSE /LON
Ticker Symbol: GSK

As of 2011, Berkshire owns 1,510,000 shares of Glaxo-SmithKline's outstanding shares—the shares are ADRs and trade on the NYSE. (ADR stands for American Depository Receipts, which is a way for foreign stocks to trade in the United States without having to file a full registration with the SEC.) With GlaxoSmithKline trading at $40 a share, Berkshire's position is worth approximately $60.4 million. With a cost of approximately $75.5 million, Berkshire has a loss of $15.1 million on this investment. This loss is reflective of recent declining stock market prices. However, the underlying economics are very strong, which makes GSK even more attractive as a long-term investment.

GlaxoSmithKline is the world's third largest manufacturer and seller of pharmaceuticals, biologics, consumer health care products, and vaccines as measured by revenues.

GSK was formed in 2000 by the merger of GlaxoWellcome plc and SmithKline Beecham plc, both companies with home offices in Great Britain. GlaxoWellcome was formed by the merger of Glaxo, founded in New Zealand in 1904, and Burroughs Wellcome & Company, founded in London in 1880. SmithKline Beecham was formed by the merger of

Smith, Kline & Co., a U.S. company founded in 1865, and the Beecham Group, which was formed in England in 1843. All these businesses have been around for more than a hundred years and have consolidated to form an economic global giant.

THE VACCINE BUSINESS

In the pharmaceutical world of economic durable competitive advantages, having a patent on a best-selling drug is about as good as it gets. The next best thing is having a monopoly on selling a country's national health program the vaccines it needs for its childhood inoculation programs. Both of these businesses are hugely profitable and GSK excels in both these categories.

The vaccine business is particularly attractive because an individual shot (or jab) costs GSK approximately $1.50 to manufacture and it sells to national vaccine programs for approximately $9 a shot. That gives GSK a net profit of approximately $7.50 a shot. This markup gives GSK a very healthy profit margin that improves with each and every new disease that the company develops a vaccine for. Consider this: GSK's profits rose 10% with the 2009 Swine Flu outbreak—a disease for which the company had a state-of-the-art vaccine ready to inoculate the masses.

In addition to its patents and the durable competitive

advantage GSK has with the vaccines, it also established the relationships with the world's governments, and it has the financial capital to create, manufacture, and sell vaccines on a world scale. If you were in charge of the health of a nation's 30 million-plus children, who would you buy your vaccines from? Every year? Year after year? You'd pick the biggest and the best. There are only four pharmaceutical giants that control most of the vaccine production in the world and GSK is one of them.

There is another component to the vaccine equation that also spells BIG MONEY: Every year, women all over the world give birth to approximately 133 million new babies, 4.3 million babies in the U.S. alone. With the United States Centers for Disease Control recommending that children aged birth through six receive thirty-four individual vaccine shots/ jabs, that means the market for those thirty-four vaccine shots/jabs increases every year by 4.3 million in just the U.S. alone. This in turn means that the vaccine manufacturers selling in the U.S. have the potential to earn a profit of $1.09 billion every year (4.3 million x 34 x $7.50 = $1.09 billion). Consider the number of yearly vaccines worldwide and the numbers are staggering—approximately $34 billion a year (133 million x 34 x $7.5 = $33.9 billion). After ten years, in the U.S. alone, vaccine manufacturers will see more than $10 billion in net profit. On a world scale, the number jumps to a potential $340 billion in profits.

And wait, it gets even better. With the invention of each new vaccine comes a patent that is good for twenty years and guarantees that no one else can make the vaccine. In other words, the company has a monopoly.

Even when the patents expire, other companies rarely step into the market because the major manufacturers have a permanent relationship with the government health departments of the world. This enables manufacturers to continue making the same vaccines year after year while maintaining their large profit margins even after their patents have expired.

And last but not least, vaccine manufacturers in the U.S. are completely immune from lawsuits. Back in the 1980s several bad batches of vaccines injured so many children that the resulting successful lawsuits threatened to bankrupt the manufacturers, so the manufacturers lobbied a bill through Congress making them a protected class.

PRESCRIPTION DRUGS

On the prescription drug side GSK's flagship products include Paxil, Wellbutrin, Zofran, Augmentin, and Valtrex, all of which have seen their patents lapse. This means GSK is now going to see competition from generic drugs. But the company manufactures many brand-name drugs that generate large amounts of income and it has an army of scientists and researchers looking for new drugs. Though a lot of press is given to drugs going off patent, at the end of the day many patients continue to ask for these brand-name drugs even though there are cheaper substitutes available. GSK asthma medication Advair is one such drug. GSK is imbedding the Advair brand name in consumer/patients' minds through the use of TV advertising. This results in patients asking their doctors for Advair by name, which means a recurring stream of income for GSK as people keep renewing their prescriptions. In 2010 alone, Advair generated $8 billion in sales.

Here is a list of GSK's many brand-name products that add to its bottom line every year:

Advair	Avodart
Albenza	BC Powder
Alli	Beano
Amerge	Beconase
Amoxil	Biotene
Aquafresh	Boniva
Arixtra	Boost
Arranon	Ceftin
Augmentin	Coreg
Avandia	Coreg CR

Dexedrine

Flixonase

Geritol

Gly-Oxide

Goody's Powder

Horlicks

Imitrex

Keppra

Lamictal

Lanoxin

Levitra (Bayer healthcare)

Lovaza

Lucozade

Macleans (toothpaste)

Nicoderm

Nicorette

NiQuitin

Panadol

Panadol night

Pandemrix

Parnate

Parodontax

Paxil

Promacta

Ralgex

Relenza

Requip

Ribena

Sensodyne

Serlipet

Setlers

Tagamet

Treximet

Trizivir

Tums

Twinrix

Tykerb

Valtrex

Ventolin HFA

Veramyst

Vesicare

Wellbutrin

Zantac

Zofran

Zovirax

GlaxoSmithKline's
Net Per Share Earnings Growth

The net per share earnings growth of a company has always been one of Warren's tests for whether or not the company in question has a durable competitive advantage. He looks for strength and consistency, which GlaxoSmithKline shows, with the exception of 2010, when restructuring charges (read downsizing and terminating repetitive jobs) drove net earnings down to $0.99 a share. The next year, per share earnings popped right back up to $3.80 a share.

From 2001 to 2011 GSK showed a 163% increase in earnings per share—and it never had a losing year, growing at a compounding annual rate of 10.19% for the last ten years.

Year	EPS (Earnings Per Share, $)
'11	3.80
'10	0.99
'09	3.38
'08	3.26
'07	3.74
'06	3.50
'05	2.98
'04	2.74
'03	2.52
'02	1.98
'01	1.44

With per share earnings in 2011 of $3.80 and an asking price of $40 a share, we can calculate that we are earning an after–corporate tax initial rate of return of $3.80, or 9.5%; and we can see that that 9.5% initial rate of return will grow at an annual rate of approximately 10.19%.

PER SHARE BOOK VALUE HISTORY

From 2001 to 2011 GSK showed a 72% increase in per share book value—growing at a compounding annual rate of 5.62% for the last ten years. One of the reasons for the low annual growth in book value (5.62%), relative to its annual earnings growth rate (10.19%), is that GSK doesn't need to retain a lot of its net profit to grow its per share earnings, so what it doesn't spend on capital improvements it pays out as a dividend.

YEAR	BVPS (Book Value Per Share, $)
'11	6.20
'10	5.24
'09	6.21
'08	5.21
'07	6.98
'06	6.53
'05	4.69
'04	4.15
'03	4.76
'02	3.58
'01	3.59

In 2011 GSK had a per share book value of $6.20 a share and was earning approximately $3.80 a share. As an equity bond, it is earning an annual rate of return of 61.2%, which is one amazing equity bond.

Since we can't buy GSK at its per share book value of $6.20 a share, we have to pay the stock market price in 2011 of approximately $40 a share. This means we can argue that we are going to be earning an after–corporate tax initial rate of return on our GSK equity bond of 9.5% ($3.80 ÷ $40 = 9.5%), but that initial after–corporate tax rate of return will increase as the company increases its earnings, which we are projecting will be at the per share historical annual rate of 10.19%.

The next question is what will a $3.80 initial after–corporate tax rate of return growing at an annual rate of approximately 10.19% look like in ten years? To help us determine this future value, we need to use the Future Value Calculator located on the Internet at http://www.investopedia.com/calculator/FVCal.aspx

Plug in: 10.19% for the Interest Rate Per Time Period; $3.80 for the Present Value; and 10 for the number of Time Periods; then click the calculate button and get $10.03. This means we can project that in 2021 GlaxoSmithKline will be earning $10.03 a share.

Now what will that $10.03 a share in earnings be worth to us in 2021? That all depends on what price-to-earnings ratio the stock market is valuing the stock at in 2021. If it is at its 2011 P/E ratio of 11 (the ten-year low), then we can project that the stock will be trading at $110.33 a share (11 x $10.03 = $110.33) in 2021. If we bought GSK stock at $40 a share in 2011 and sold it for $110.33 a share in 2021, our total gain on the sale would be $70.33 a share, giving us a total return of 175% and a compounding annual rate of return of 10.68% for the ten-year period.

Though GlaxoSmithKline has raised its dividend almost every year for the last ten years, if it can just maintain its 2011 dividend of $2.08 a share until 2021, we can add in $20.80 to our $110.33 proceeds from the sale, boosting our combined sale proceeds and dividends up to $131.13. This increases our total return to 227% and our compounding annual rate of return to 12.61%.

Now does a projected compounding annual rate of return of 12.61% for ten years get you interested? Warren bought $75.5 million worth of GlaxoSmithKline stock because he found a 12.61% compounding annual rate of return for ten or more years to be a very attractive investment. Even if over the short term he shows a loss in the investment.

CHAPTER 13

Johnson & Johnson

Address:
One Johnson & Johnson Plaza
New Brunswick, New Jersey 08933 USA
Telephone: (732) 524-0400
Website: http://www.jnj.com

Industry: Pharmaceutical/Health Care and Consumer
Products

Key Statistics:
Public Company
Founded in 1887
Employees: 114,000
Sales: $65 billion (2011)
Net Earnings: $13.7 billion (2011)
Per Share Earnings: $4.95 (2011)
Average Annual Growth for Per Share Earnings: 9.99%
Per Share Book Value: $23.05
Average Annual Growth for Per Share Book Value: 11.23%
Dividend/Yield 2011: $2.28/3.4%
Years of Berkshire Purchase: 2006, 2007, 2010
Average Per Share Price Berkshire Paid: $60.85
Stock Exchanges: NYSE
Ticker Symbol: JNJ

As of 2011, Berkshire owns 45,022,563 shares, or 1.6% of Johnson & Johnson's outstanding shares. With Johnson & Johnson trading at $65 a share, Berkshire's position is worth approximately $2.93 billion; with a cost of $2.749 billion, Berkshire has a profit of $181 million on this investment.

Johnson & Johnson is a global manufacturer and seller of pharmaceuticals, medical supplies, and dozens of everyday brand-name consumer products. It has been in business since 1887 and one of its early brand-name products that came to own a piece of consumers' minds was Johnson's Baby Powder, and later Johnson's Baby Oil. These products created the wealth to develop and market such everyday household staples as Band-Aid bandages, Motrin and Tylenol, Neutrogena skin and beauty products, AVEENO, and the brands Listerine and Benadryl. Johnson & Johnson employs over 114,000 people and has 250 companies operating in more than 60 countries.

The key for Warren is the brand-name products. Listerine, Band-Aid bandages, Motrin, and Tylenol are going to be around for a long, long time and the plants and equipment that are producing them have to be replaced only when the parts wear out. This creates far better long-term economics than, say, the auto industry, where companies have to go in every few years and spend hundreds of millions on research and development and retooling their plants to produce the latest model.

JOHNSON & JOHNSON'S
INTERNATIONAL TAX ADVANTAGE

One advantage that an international company like Johnson & Johnson can offer the long-term investor over domestic U.S. companies is that the profits on its overseas operations aren't taxed until Johnson & Johnson brings them back into the U.S.—which it tends not to do. But it does get to report those profits on its income statement as soon as they are earned, so the market can take into account the value they add to the company. Think of it as Johnson & Johnson getting to defer paying taxes on its overseas income forever if it wishes. This means that all that money that would have gone to pay taxes gets added to the pool of overseas capital, which means the company has even more money to grow its foreign operations. Which helps explain why J&J's ten-year average compounding growth rate for international sales grew at a rate of 10.5%, compared to U.S. sales growth of only 5.5% for the same period. In J&J's 2011 10-K filed with the Securities and Exchange Commission, it reported that:

At January 2, 2011 and January 3, 2010, the cumulative amounts of undistributed international earnings were approximately $37.0 billion and $32.2 billion, respectively. The Company intends to continue to reinvest its undistributed international earnings to expand its international operations; therefore, no U.S. tax expense has been recorded with respect to the undistributed portion not intended for repatriation.

This means that out of J&J's $77 billion in retained earnings, approximately 48% of them are held overseas out of the clutches of the U.S. taxing authorities and are free to grow unimpeded by the effects of U.S. taxes.

To understand the power that this abatement of taxes can have on increasing the value of a company, consider this: J&J earns on average a 10% rate of return on assets. If over the next ten years it earns a 10% compounding annual rate of return on the $37 billion it held overseas at the end of 2010, then by 2020 its pool of undistributed international earnings will have grown to be worth a little better than $100 billion. If it had to pay U.S. federal and state taxes on what it earned on that amount, its pool of undistributed international earnings would have grown only to around $65 billion. Which means we can argue that the international tax advantage that J&J has will have helped its shareholders become approximately $35 billion richer, which was equal to about 62% of J&J's net worth of $56 billion in 2010.

When you think of the international tax advantage, think of compounding on steroids. Since Warren is all about long-term growth, this international tax advantage is important. He knows that it greatly adds to Johnson & Johnson's long-term earnings growth, and that will eventually lead to the long-term growth of the underlying value of the company, which the stock market will recognize by bidding up the price of its shares.

Johnson & Johnson's
Net Per Share Earnings Growth

From 2001 to 2011 Johnson & Johnson showed a 159% increase in earnings per share—and it never had a losing year, growing at a compounding annual rate of 9.99% for the last ten years.

Year	EPS (Earnings Per Share, $)
'11	4.95
'10	4.76
'09	4.63
'08	4.57
'07	4.15
'06	3.76
'05	3.50
'04	3.10
'03	2.70
'02	2.23
'01	1.91

With per share earnings in 2011 of $4.95 and an asking price of $65 a share, we can argue that we are earning an after–corporate tax initial rate of return of $4.95, or 7.6%; and we can argue that that 7.6% initial rate of turn will grow at its historic annual per share earnings growth rate of approximately 9.99%.

Per Share Book Value History

From 2001 to 2011 Johnson & Johnson showed a 189% increase in per share book value—and it never had a losing year, growing at a compounding annual rate of 11.23% for the last ten years.

Year	BVPS (Book Value Per Share, $)
'11	23.05
'10	20.66
'09	18.37
'08	15.35
'07	15.25
'06	13.59
'05	12.73
'04	10.71
'03	9.05
'02	7.65
'01	7.95

In 2011 Johnson & Johnson was earning approximately $4.95 a share and had a per share book value of $23.05 a share. This means that our Johnson & Johnson equity bond is earning an annual rate of return of 21.4% ($4.95 ÷ $23.05 = 21.4%). But we can't buy it at its per share book value of $23.05; we have to pay the stock market price in 2011 of approximately $65 a share. This means we can project that we are going to be earning an after–corporate tax initial rate of return on our Johnson & Johnson equity bond of 7.6% ($4.95 ÷ $65 = 7.6%). That initial after–corporate tax rate of return, however, will increase as the company increases its earnings, which we are projecting will be at its per share earnings historical annual rate of 9.99%.

The next question is what will a $4.95 initial after–corporate tax rate of return growing at an annual rate of approximately 9.99% look like in ten years? To help us determine this future value we need to use the Future Value Calculator located on the Internet at http://www.investopedia.com/calculator/FVCal.aspx

Plug in: 9.99% for the Interest Rate Per Time Period; $4.95 for the Present Value; and 10 for the number of Time Periods; then click the calculate button to get $12.83. Which means that if we pay $65 for a share of Johnson & Johnson stock, by

2021 it will be earning an after–corporate tax $12.83, which equates to a 19.7% return for a $65-a-share investment.

Now what will that $12.83 a share be worth to us in 2021? That all depends on what price-to-earnings ratio the stock market is valuing the stock at in 2021. If it is at its 2011 P/E ratio of 12 (which also is its ten-year historic low), then we can project that the stock will be trading at $153.96 a share by 2021.

If we bought Johnson & Johnson stock at $65 a share in 2011 and sold it for $153.96 a share in 2021, our total gain from the sale would be $88.96 a share, giving us a total return of 136.8% and a compounding annual rate of return of 9.01% for the ten-year period.

Though Johnson & Johnson has raised its dividend every year for the last ten years, if it can just maintain its 2011 dividend of $2.28 a share until 2021, we can add $22.80 to our $153.96 proceeds from the sale, boosting the proceeds from the sale and dividends combined up to $176.76, which increases our total return to 171% and our compounding annual rate of return to 10.52%.

Does a projected compounding annual rate of return of 10.52% for ten years perk up your ears? For Warren it is perky enough for him to keep $2.93 billion in Johnson & Johnson stock.

CHAPTER 14

Kraft Foods, Inc.

Address:
Three Lakes Drive
Northfield, IL 60093 USA
Telephone: (847) 646-2000
Website: http://www.kraft.com

Industry: Confectionery, Food, and Beverage

Key Statistics:
Public Company
Founded in 1903
Employees: 97,000
Sales: $52.5 billion (2011)
Net Earnings: $4.1 billion (2011)
Per Share Earnings: $2.20 (2011)
Average Annual Growth for Per Share Earnings: 6.52%
Per Share Book Value: $22.50
Average Annual Growth for Per Share Book Value: 5.22%
Dividend/Yield 2011: $1.16/3.3%
Years of Berkshire Purchase: 2007, 2008
Average Per Share Price Berkshire Paid: $32.91
Stock Exchanges: NYSE
Ticker Symbol: KFT

As of 2011, Berkshire owns 97,214,514 shares, or 5.6% of Kraft Foods' outstanding shares. With Kraft trading at $35 a share, Berkshire's position is worth approximately $3.4 billion; with a cost of $3.2 billion, Berkshire has a profit of approximately $200 million on this investment.

Kraft is the largest food and beverage company in the United States, and it is the second largest in the world. That's big. We're talking Kraft cheese, Cadbury candy, Maxwell House and Jacobs Coffees, Nabisco cookies and crackers, Philadelphia Cream Cheese, Oscar Mayer meats, and more. Kraft markets brands in more than 180 countries and 40 of its brands are more than a hundred years old. This is exactly what Warren is looking for—consistent products that never have to be upgraded to keep them competitive. No "technological breakthrough" is ever going to render Kraft's Nabisco Oreo cookie obsolete. A hundred years from now, children will still be tearing apart those chocolate-cream delights and licking off the icing with smiles on their little faces.

Warren likes his companies old and very successful, and with Kraft he gets both. Started in 1903, by James L. Kraft and his four brothers, as a wholesale door-to-door cheese business in Chicago, the company soon took hold. In 1912 Kraft established its U.S. headquarters in New York City. By 1914 it had thirty-one different kinds of cheese that it was selling around the U.S. But Kraft's fortunes really started to increase in 1915, when it invented and patented a process for making pasteurized cheese. This allowed Kraft to sell close to six million pounds of canned cheese to the U.S. Army for rations during World War I and gave a million or more American servicemen a taste for Kraft cheese.

The 1920s was a period of growing the company by acquisition: in 1927, A. E. Wright salad dressings; and in 1928, Phenix Cheese, Southern Dairies, and Henard Mayonnaise. In 1929 Kraft acquired fifteen different companies, including three other mayonnaise manufacturers. By 1930 it had 40% of the cheese market in the U.S. and had become its third largest dairy. Velveeta was introduced in 1928 and was an instant success because it could melt easily. Velveeta macaroni and cheese instantly became a household favorite.

In the 1930s Kraft merged with National Dairy, making it the largest dairy operation in the U.S. During World War II Kraft was sending twenty million pounds of cheese to Great Britain each month, setting the stage for the creation of a European market for Kraft's products.

In 1947 the company tested selling cheese on a new invention called the television via the *Kraft Television Theatre* program. The first cheese tested was a new product that had never been advertised before, and even though there was no other advertising support for it, the stores could not keep up with the demand created by the TV ads. Advertising on TV really worked.

In the 1950s Kraft brought to market packaged cheese slices and Cheez Whiz. The 1960s saw the introduction of Kraft Singles—individually wrapped cheese slices. It also introduced Kraft fruit preserves, marshmallows, and barbecue sauces. Kraft also started to make its big push into worldwide markets in the 1960s and 1970s.

The early 1980s saw Kraft merge with Dart Industries— the makers of Duracell Batteries, West Bend home appliances, and Tupperware plastic containers. It also acquired KitchenAid appliances, Lender's Bagels, and Celestial Seasonings tea.

Later in the 1980s Kraft either spun off its nonfood businesses to its shareholders or, as with the case of Duracell, in 1988 sold it to the private equity firm Kohlberg Kravis & Roberts.

The tobacco company Philip Morris purchased Kraft at the end of 1988 for $12.9 billion and merged it with its General Foods division, which included the brands Oscar Mayer meats, Maxwell House coffee, Jell-O gelatin, Budget Gourmet frozen dinners, Entenmann's baked goods, and Kool-Aid, Crystal Light, and Tang powdered beverage mixes. In 1990 Philip Morris acquired the European coffee and candy maker Jacobs Suchard.

In 2000 Philip Morris acquired international food giant Nabisco Holdings for $18.9 billion and merged Nabisco into Kraft the same year.

In 2007 Philip Morris (now called Altria) decided that the stigma of its tobacco business was causing the stock market to place a lower valuation on its Kraft food group, so Philip Morris decided to spin off Kraft/General Foods to its shareholders to unlock Kraft's true value for Altria's owners. It was a two-step process, with Philip Morris first selling 16% of Kraft to the public, which it did in the fall of 2007 at a market valuation of approximately $60 billion.

In 2008 Berkshire Hathaway announced that it had acquired 8% of Kraft's total outstanding shares for approximately $4 billion. It was also announced that Warren's business partner Charlie Munger had acquired $300 million of Kraft's stock for his own personal account.

In 2010 Kraft bought the British confectionery company Cadbury for $16.2 billion, making Kraft-Cadbury the second largest confectionery manufacturer in the world, right behind Nestlé, the most diversified and largest food company in the world.

LET'S LOOK AT THE NUMBERS

If we look at Kraft's per share earnings history we can see that from 2001 to 2011 it showed an 88% increase in earnings per share and an overall annual compounding growth rate of

6.52% for the last ten years. During the banking crisis, people still had to eat and Kraft's earnings stayed strong and steady. Warren likes strong and steady earnings.

Year	EPS (Earnings Per Share, $)
'11	2.20
'10	2.02
'09	2.03
'08	1.88
'07	1.82
'06	1.94
'05	1.88
'04	1.87
'03	2.00
'02	2.02
'01	1.17

With Kraft's per share earnings in 2011 at $2.20 and an asking price of $35 a share, we are earning an after–corporate tax initial rate of return of $2.20 or 6.28% ($2.20 ÷ $35 = 6.28%); and we predict that that 6.28% initial rate of return will grow at an annual rate of 6.52%. Is that an interest return for you? If Kraft can keep it up over time, its stock value will also rise to reflect the increase in per share earnings and underlying per share book value.

Per Share Book Value History

From 2001 to 2011 Kraft Foods showed a 66% increase in per share book value—growing at a compounding annual rate of 5.22% for the last ten years.

Year	BVPS (Book Value Per Share, $)
'11	22.50
'10	20.30
'09	17.57
'08	15.11
'07	17.80
'06	17.45
'05	17.72
'04	17.54
'03	16.57
'02	14.93
'01	13.53

In 2011 Kraft Foods had a per share book value of $22.50 a share and was earning approximately $2.20 a share. Which means that we can argue that as an equity bond, it is earning an annual rate of return of 9.7%. But we can't buy it at its per share book value of $22.50; we have to pay the stock market price in 2011 of approximately $35 a share. That means we can argue that we are going to be earning an initial rate of return on our Kraft equity bond of 6.28%, but that initial after–corporate tax rate of return will increase on an annual basis at a rate of 6.52%.

The next question is what will a $2.20 initial after–corporate tax rate of return growing at an annual rate of 6.52% look like in ten years? Let's use the Future Value Calculator located on the Internet at http://www.investopedia.com/calculator/FVCal.aspx

Plug in: 6.52% for the Interest Rate Per Time Period; $2.20 for the Present Value; and 10 for the number of Time Periods; then click the calculate button to get $4.14. Which means that if we pay $35 for a share of Kraft stock, by 2021 it will earn $4.14 a share, which equates to a 13.4% return on our $35-a-share investment.

Now what will that $4.14 a share be worth to us in 2021? That all depends on what price-to-earnings ratio the stock market is valuing the stock at in 2021. If it is at its 2011 P/E ratio of 12.8 (its ten-year low), then we can project that the stock will be trading at $52.99 a share. If we bought Kraft stock at $35 a share in 2011 and sold it for $52.99 a share in 2021, our total gain from the sale would be $17.99 a share, giving us a total return of 51% and a compounding annual rate of return of 4.23% for the ten-year period.

Though Kraft has consistently raised its dividend over the last ten years, if it can just maintain its 2011 dividend of $1.16 a share till 2021, then we can add in $11.60 to our $52.99 gross proceeds from the sale, boosting our proceeds from the sale and dividends up to $64.59, which increases our total return to 84.54% and our compounding annual rate of return to 6.32%.

Does a projected 6.32% annual compounding rate of return for ten years seem an attractive investment for you? For Warren it was attractive enough to buy $3.2 billion worth of Kraft's stock.

CHAPTER 15

Moody's Corporation

Address:
7 World Trade Center
250 Greenwich Street
New York, NY 10007 USA
Telephone: (212) 553-0300
Website: http://www.moodys.com

Industry: Financial Ratings Agency

Key Statistics:
Public Company
Founded in 1900
Employees: 3,900
Revenue: $2.3 billion (2011)
Net Earnings: $560 million (2011)
Per Share Earnings: $2.45 (2011)
Average Annual Growth for Per Share Earnings: 14.02%
Per Share Book Value: $0.55–Negative
Average Annual Growth for Per Share Book Value: 0%
Dividend/Yield 2011: $0.56/1.75%
Year of Berkshire Purchase: 2010
Average Per Share Price Berkshire Paid: $20.79
Stock Exchanges: NYSE
Ticker Symbol: MCO

As of 2011, Berkshire owns 28,414,000 shares of Moody's outstanding shares (approximately 12%). With Moody's trading at $32 a share, Berkshire's position is worth approximately $909 million; with a cost of approximately $284 million, Berkshire has a profit of $625.2 million on this investment.

Moody's Corporation owns two separate businesses. One is Moody's Analytics, which provides capital markets and risk management professionals with credit analysis, economic research, financial-risk management software, and advisory services, and produces approximately $600 million in revenue. The other business is Moody's Investor Service, a credit rating agency that does international financial research and analysis on commercial and governmental bond issuers. It is this business that rates the creditworthiness of issuers of debt and generates the majority of its revenue. Presently Moody's controls approximately 40% of the world credit rating market. The other big players are Standard & Poor's and Fitch Ratings.

Moody's was founded in 1909 by John Moody when he published an investment manual entitled "Analysis of Railroad Investments," which provided risk assessment for different railroad bonds. By 1914, the company had expanded into rating municipal bonds, and by 1924 it covered nearly

100% of the U.S. bond market. In the 1970s it expanded into commercial and international debt and started charging bond issuers to rate their debt; previously, it had charged only investors seeking the information.

Out of all the businesses that Warren invests in, Moody's is probably the most profitable for the capital employed. Its operating margins consistently rank between 45% and 55%—compare that to Coca-Cola's 31% or Johnson & Johnson's 32%—and its net profits are strong and consistent even in the worst economic environments.

One of the oddities of Moody's business is that it has a net income of $500-plus million a year, yet it has a negative per share book value. How can this be? Moody's is such an exceptional business that it doesn't need much in the way of assets to make money—basically office space, computers, and equipment for 3,600 people, and that is about it. Total plant and equipment comes in at $535 million, which means that in any given year it earns enough to replicate itself as needed. Its total assets are $2.5 billion and total liabilities, $2.7 billion, which basically gives the company a negative net worth of approximately $200 million. What keeps it going is its rock-solid income stream and the excess capital it throws off year after year.

So what happens to all the money it makes? A small part of it is paid out in dividends, but the other part is mostly used to aggressively buy back its own stock. From 2001 to 2011 it bought back 76 million shares at a cost of approximately $4.4 billion.

MOODY'S NET PER SHARE EARNINGS GROWTH

From 2001 to 2011, Moody's showed a 271% increase in earnings per share—and it never had a losing year, growing at a compounding annual rate of 14.02% for the last ten years.

YEAR	EPS (Earnings Per Share, $)
'11	2.45
'10	1.97
'09	1.69
'08	1.86
'07	2.50
'06	2.25
'05	1.82
'04	1.50
'03	1.17
'02	0.92
'01	0.66

With per share earnings in 2011 of $2.45 and an asking price of $32 a share, we can argue that we are earning an after–corporate tax initial rate of return of $2.45, or 7.6%;

and we can state that that 7.6% initial rate of return will grow at its historic per share earnings annual growth rate of approximately 14.02%.

The next question is, what will a $2.45-a-share initial after–corporate rate of return growing at an annual rate of approximately 14.02% look like in ten years? Use the Future Value Calculator located on the Internet at http://www .investopedia.com/calculator/FVCal.aspx to help determine this future value.

Plug in: 14.02% for the Interest Rate Per Time Period; $2.45 for the Present Value; and 10 for the number of Time Periods; then click the calculate button to get $9.10. Which means that if we pay $32 for a share of Moody's stock in 2011, by 2021 it will be earning approximately $9.10 a share.

Now what will that $9.10 be worth to us in 2021? That all depends on what price-to-earnings ratio the stock market is valuing the stock at in 2021. If it is at its 2011 P/E ratio of 12 (its ten-year low), then we can project that the stock will be trading at $109.20 a share ($9.10 x 12 = $109.20). If we bought Moody's stock at $32 a share in 2011 and sold it for $109.20 a share in 2021, our total gain from the sale would be $77.20 a share, giving us a total return of 241% and an annual rate of return of 13.06% for the ten-year period.

Though Moody's has raised its dividend every year for the last ten years, if it can just maintain its 2011 dividend of $0.52 a share till 2021, we can add $5.20 to our $109.20

proceeds from the sale, boosting proceeds from sale and dividends combined up to $114.40. That increases our total return to 257% and our compounding annual rate of return to 13.59%.

So how do you feel about earning a potential 13.59% compounding annual rate of return for ten years? Warren feels strongly enough about it to keep $909 million of Berkshire's money in Moody's stock.

CHAPTER 16

Procter & Gamble Company

Address:
1 Procter & Gamble Plaza
Cincinnati, OH 45202 USA
Telephone: (513) 983-1100
Website: http://www.pg.com

Industry: Worldwide Consumer Products

Key Statistics:
Public Company
Founded in 1837
Employees: 127,000
Sales: $82 billion (2011)
Net Earnings: $11.9 billion (2011)
Per Share Earnings: $3.98 (2011)
Average Annual Growth for Per Share Earnings: 9.82%
Per Share Book Value: $22.10
Average Annual Growth for Per Share Book Value: 18.7%
Dividend/Yield 2011: $2.10/3.3%
Year of Berkshire Purchase: 2005 via P&G's acquisition
   of Gillette
Average Per Share Price Berkshire Paid: $6.40
Stock Exchanges: NYSE
Ticker Symbol: PG

As of 2011, Berkshire owns 72,391,036 shares, or 2.6% of Procter & Gamble's outstanding shares. With P&G trading at $61 a share, Berkshire's position is worth approximately $4.4 billion; with a cost of $464 million, Berkshire has a profit of approximately $3.9 billion on this investment.

Procter & Gamble is a global manufacturer and seller of almost every product that we find in the household bathroom and laundry. Just look at the stunning array of brand-name products it has in its product portfolio:

Ariel—a brand laundry detergent

Bounty—a high-end paper towel

Braun—a worldwide manufacturer of small appliances

CoverGirl—a leading brand of women's cosmetics

Crest/Oral B—a top brand of toothpaste and toothbrushes

Dawn/Fairy—major brand of dishwashing liquid

Downey—fabric softener for the wash

Duracell—top battery sold in seventy-five countries

Fusion—an emerging brand of shavers

Gillette—the world's leading manufacturer of shaving razors

Head & Shoulders—the top-selling dandruff shampoo

Olay—leading brand of women's skin-care products

Pampers—top-selling brand of diapers

Tide—worldwide brand laundry detergent

Now you're starting to get the picture: P&G provides the products that people use every day in the world's bathrooms and laundry rooms all over the world, products that are bought and used up on a daily basis. The world consumes 25 billion batteries a year and P&G's subsidiary Duracell is the world's leading manufacturer. P&G's Gillette has 70% of the global market for razors and blades. This means that every day a billion or more people get up in the morning and use P&G's products—products that wear out quickly and have to be replaced after, products that have a tremendous amount of consumer loyalty. Tide, P&G's laundry detergent brand, has 40% of the North American market, and with $2.4 billion in sales, Tide would qualify as a Fortune 500 company all by itself. Many of P&G's products have been best sellers for decades. With manufacturing operations all over the world— thirty-one manufacturing plants in China alone—P&G is a giant in the global consumer products market.

History of the Company

P&G was founded in Cincinnati in 1837 by William Procter— an English candlemaker—and James Gamble—an Irish soap maker—who met when they married a pair of Cincinnati gals by the names of Olivia and Elizabeth Norris. The Norris girls' father, Alexander Norris, was a local businessman who saw a great future in candles and soap (soap turned out to be the better business) and persuaded his two sons-in-law to go into business with each other by putting up their initial capital.

By 1859 P&G was doing a roaring business selling candles (there were no electric lights) and soap (tons of dirty workers building the American West), with sales reaching $1 million. In 1861 P&G became the preferred provider of candles and soap to the Union Army fighting the American Civil War.

In the 1880s P&G came up with a revolutionary new product, soap that would float! Up until then, when one took a bath, that little bar of soap sank to the bottom of the tub and lay hidden while the bather blindly felt around for it. Thanks to P&G's product scientists, soap could float in clear view on top of the water—making it easy to find. They called this soap Ivory. It sold for 10 cents a bar and was an instant success. In the 1920s P&G started sponsoring radio programs to help sell Ivory soap and in the process gave birth to what we now call "soap operas." A hundred thirty years after it was invented, Ivory soap is a very popular brand—all over the world.

P&G's international expansion began in the 1930s with the acquisition of the Thomas Hedley Company, the largest English candle and soap manufacturer. P&G also started to launch new products. In 1947 it started selling Tide laundry detergent, which turned into a top-selling world brand. In 1957 P&G brought to market a new brand of toothpaste with fluoride it called Crest, and it also bought the Charmin Paper Mills and started making and selling toilet paper and paper kitchen towels. In 1961 it launched Pampers disposable diapers and freed babies and parents the world over from those terrible cloth diapers that had to be washed every time they were used.

In 2005 P&G acquired razor blade manufacturer Gillette, and with it came the brands Duracell and Braun. In the process P&G became the largest consumer goods company in the world.

PROCTER & GAMBLE'S
INTERNATIONAL TAX ADVANTAGE

P&G benefits from the same international tax advantage that Johnson & Johnson does. In 2011 P&G reported that it had $30 billion in overseas profits that it was keeping overseas to protect it from U.S. taxes. This means that out of the $70 billion in retained earnings found on P&G's balance sheet, approximately 42% of it is held overseas free to grow unimpeded by the punitive effects of U.S. taxes. That's a considerable advantage that over the longterm can create considerable shareholder value. (For a full discussion on the benefits of the international tax advantage, please refer back to the Johnson & Johnson chapter.)

Procter & Gamble's
Net Per Share Earnings Growth

From 2001 to 2011 Procter & Gamble showed a 155% increase in earnings per share—and it never had a losing year, growing at a compounding annual rate of 9.82% for the last ten years.

Year	EPS (Earnings Per Share, $)
'11	3.98
'10	3.53
'09	3.58
'08	3.64
'07	3.04
'06	2.76
'05	2.53
'04	2.32
'03	2.04
'02	1.80
'01	1.56

With per share earnings in 2011 of $3.98 and an asking price of $61 a share, we can argue that we are earning an after–corporate tax initial rate of return of $3.98, or 6.5%; and we can state that that 6.5% initial rate of return will grow at an annual rate of approximately 9.82%.

Per Share Book Value History

From 2001 to 2011 Procter & Gamble showed a 455% increase in per share book value—growing at a compounding annual rate of 18.7% for the last ten years.

Year	BVPS (Book Value Per Share, $)
'11	22.10
'10	21.20
'09	21.18
'08	22.46
'07	20.87
'06	19.33
'05	6.47
'04	6.19
'03	5.63
'02	4.64
'01	3.98

In 2011 Procter & Gamble had a per share book value of $22.10 and was earning approximately $3.98 a share. Which means that from Warren's perspective, as an equity bond, it is earning an annual rate of return of 18% ($3.98 ÷ $22.10 = 18%).

But we can't buy it at its per share book value of $22.10; we have to pay the stock market price in 2011 of approximately $61 a share. That means we can argue that we are going to be earning an after–corporate tax initial rate of return on our Procter & Gamble equity bond of 6.5% ($3.98 ÷ $61 = 6.5%), but that initial after–corporate tax rate of return will increase as the company increases its earnings, which we are projecting will be at their historic per share annual rate of 9.82%.

The next question is what will a $3.98 initial after–corporate tax rate of return growing at an annual rate of approximately 9.82% look like in ten years? To answer that, we use the Future Value Calculator located on the Internet at http://www.investopedia.com/calculator/FVCal.aspx

Plug in: 9.82% for the Interest Rate Per Time Period; $3.98 for the Present Value; and 10 for the number of Time Periods; then click the calculate button to get $10.16. Which means that in 2021 Procter & Gamble will be earning $10.16 a share.

Now what will that $10.16 be worth to us in 2021? That all depends on what price-to-earnings ratio the stock market is valuing the stock at in 2021. If it is at its 2011 P/E ratio of 16.4 (which is its ten-year historic low), we can project that the stock will be trading at $166.62 a share. If we bought Procter & Gamble stock at $61 a share in 2011 and sold it for $166.62 a share in 2021, our total gain from the sale would be $105.62 a share, giving us a total return of 173% and an annual rate of return of 10.57% for the ten-year period.

Though Procter & Gamble has raised its dividend every

year for the last ten years, if it can just maintain its 2011 dividend of $2.10 a share till 2021, we can add $21.00 to our $166.62 proceeds from the sale, boosting our proceeds from sale and dividends combined to $187.62, which increases our total return to 207% and our annual rate of return to 11.89%.

How does a projected compounding annual rate of return of 11.89% for ten years sound to you? With Warren keeping $4.4 billion invested in Procter & Gamble shares, you can make a good guess at how it sounds to him.

CHAPTER 17

Sanofi S.A.

France Address:
174 Avenue de France
Paris 75013
France

U.S. Address:
55 Corporate Drive
Bridgewater, NJ 08807 USA
U.S. Telephone: (908) 981-5560
Website: http://www.sanofi.com

Industry: Pharmaceutical / Health Care

Key Statistics:
Public Company
Founded in 1973
Employees: 101,575
Sales: $45.7 billion (2011)
Net Earnings: $7.6 billion (2011)
Per Share Earnings: $2.90 (2011) ADR
Average Annual Growth for Per Share Earnings: 12.52%
Per Share Book Value: $29.00 ADR
Average Annual Growth for Per Share Book Value: 4.17%
Dividend/Yield 2011: $1.76/5.36%ADR
Years of Berkshire Purchase: 2007, 2008, 2009

Average Per Share Price Berkshire Paid: $79 Ordinary Shares /
$39.50 ADR
Sanofi shares trade in the U.S. as ADRs, with each ADR repre-
senting one half of one share of ordinary Sanofi common
stock. The Sanofi ADRs trade on the NYSE under the
ticker symbol: SNY.
Sanofi ordinary common shares also trade on the Paris
exchange, in Euros, under the ticker symbol SAN.PA.

As of 2011, Berkshire owns 25,848,838 shares of Sanofi
outstanding shares with a cost of $2.06 billion. With Sanofi
ordinary shares trading at the U.S. equivalent of $70 a share
($34 for the ADR), Berkshire's position is worth approxi-
mately $1.809 billion, giving Warren a loss of $251 million.

Sanofi is the third largest pharmaceutical company in the
world, behind Pfizer and GlaxoSmithKline, on the basis of
prescription sales. While the origins of the company date
back to 1973, it has grown substantially by merging with
other pharmaceutical companies, which have included Ster-
ling-Winthrop (now Sterling Drug)—a global pharmaceutical
company based in the U.S.; and Synthelabo, the pharmaceutical arm of L'Oréal, the world's largest cosmetic and beauty
company. In 2004 Sanofi acquired the vaccine giant Aventis
and in the process made Sanofi's subsidiary, Sanofi Pasteur,
the world's largest company devoted entirely to the development and sale of vaccines. In 2011 Sanofi acquired Genzyme,
the third largest biotechnology company in the world.

As we said earlier in our discussion of GlaxoSmithKline, there is no business like the vaccine business. It has constant and growing demand for its products and the profit margins are out of this world. In 2010 Sanofi Pasteur produced more than 1.6 billion doses of vaccines to immunize more than 500 million people all over the world. Out of the top four makers of vaccines it has the largest product range—covering more than twenty infectious diseases. All in all, it sold more than $5.5 billion worth of vaccines in 2011 and will continue to be a solid source of profitable income for a long time to come.

(Note to reader: The following financial numbers have been adjusted for the Sanofi ADR shares, as these ADR financial numbers are the ones our American readers will have ready access to. The ADR shares represent one half of an ordinary share of Sanofi, which is traded on the Paris Exchange.)

SANOFI'S NET PER SHARE EARNINGS GROWTH

Since the merger with Aventis in 2004, Sanofi has shown a 128% increase in earnings per share—and it has never had a losing year, growing at a compounding annual rate of 12.52% for the last seven years.

Year	EPS ADR (Earnings Per Share American Depository Receipts, $)
'11	2.90
'10	2.76
'09	3.02
'08	2.37
'07	2.38
'06	1.95
'05	1.65
'04	1.27

With per share earnings in 2011 of $2.90 and an asking price of $35 an ADR share, we can argue that we are earning an after–corporate tax initial rate of return of $2.90 a share or 8.2%; and we can state that that 8.2% initial rate of return will grow at an annual rate of approximately 12.52%.

ADR Per Share Book Value History

From 2004 to 2011 Sanofi showed a 33.1% increase in per share book value—and it has never had a losing year, growing at a compounding annual rate of 4.17% for the last seven years.

Year	BVPS (Book Value Per Share, $)
'11	27.85
'10	26.73

Year	BVPS ($)
'09	26.32
'08	23.87
'07	24.48
'06	22.34
'05	20.38
'04	20.92

Buffett Buy Analysis

In 2011 Sanofi had an ADR per share book value of $27.85 a share and was earning approximately $2.90 a share. Which means that we can argue that as an equity bond, it is earning an annual rate of return of 10.4%, which we can argue is going to grow at Sanofi's per share earnings annual growth rate of 12.52%.

But we can't buy Sanofi at its per share book value of $27.85; we have to pay the stock market price in 2011 of approximately $35 a share. That means we can argue that we are going to be earning an after–corporate tax initial rate of return on our Sanofi equity bond of 8.2% ($2.90 ÷ $35 = 8.2%). But that initial rate of return will increase as the company increases its earnings, which we are projecting will be at its historic per share annual growth rate of 12.52%.

To answer the next question—What will a $2.90 initial after?–corporate tax rate of return growing at an annual rate of approximately 12.52% look like in ten years—use the Future Value Calculator located on the Internet at http://www .investopedia.com/calculator/FVCal.aspx

Plug in: 12.52% for the Interest Rate Per Time Period; $2.90 for the Present Value; and 10 for the number of Time Periods; then click the calculate button to get $9.43. Which means that if we pay $35 for a share of Sanofi stock, by 2021 we can project that it will be earning $9.43 a share.

Now what will that $9.43 be worth to us in 2021? That all depends on what price-to-earnings ratio the stock market is valuing the stock at in 2021. If it is at its 2011 P/E ratio of 11 (which is the lowest P/E for the last seven years), we can project that the stock will be trading at $103.73 a share (11 x $9.43 = $103.73). If we bought Sanofi stock at $35 a share in 2011 and sold it for $103.73 a share in 2021, our total gain from the sale would be $68.73 a share, giving us a total return of 196% and a compounding annual rate of return of 11.48% for the ten-year period.

Though Sanofi has raised its dividend every year for the last seven years, if it can just maintain its 2011 dividend of $1.79 a share till 2021, we can add in $17.90 to our $103.73 proceeds from the sale, boosting proceeds from sale and dividends combined up to $121.63, which increases our total return to 247% and our compounding annual rate of return to 13.27%.

Does a projected compounding annual rate of return of 13.27% for ten years interest you? It is interesting enough for Warren to invest $2.06 billion in Sanofi, although he has not yet shown a profit on this investment.

CHAPTER 18

Torchmark Corporation

Address:
3700 South Stonebridge Drive
McKinney, TX 75070
Telephone: (972) 569-4000
Website: http://www.torchmarkcorp.com

Industry: Life and Property Insurance

Key Statistics:
Public Company
Founded in 1900
Employees: 2,300
Premium Income: $2.65 billion (2011)
Investment Income: $698 million (2011)
Net Earnings: $525 million (2011)
Per Share Earnings: $4.65 (2011)
Average Annual Growth for Per Share Earnings: 8.43%
Per Share Book Value: $38.10
Average Annual Growth for Per Share Book Value: 10.89%
Dividend/Yield 2011: $0.49/1.36%
Years of Berkshire Purchase: 2000, 2006
Average Per Share Price Berkshire Paid: $20.50
Stock Exchanges: NYSE
Ticker Symbol: TMK

As of 2011, Berkshire owns 2.82 million shares of Torchmark's outstanding common stock at a cost of $57.8 million. With Torchmark trading at $36 a share, Berkshire's position is worth approximately $101.5 million, giving it a profit of $43.7 million.

The core holding of Torchmark is Liberty National Life Insurance Company, which was founded in Birmingham, Alabama, in 1900 as a fraternal organization to provide benefits to its members. It became a stock company in the 1930s and over the last hundred years has grown into a business that operates in forty-nine states, with 130 branch offices and 3,000 agents. It has over $43 billion of insurance in force and 4.1 million policies.

In 1980 Liberty National acquired Global Life and Accident Insurance Company and formed the holding company Torchmark Corporation. In 1981 Torchmark acquired United Investors Life Insurance Company and United American Insurance Company. In 1992 it acquired American Income Life Insurance Company, and in 2010 it sold United Investors Life Insurance Company.

Torchmark companies have a total of $150 billion in force, $17 billion in assets, and $4 billion in shareholders' equity. Its assets are almost entirely high-grade bonds and in 2011 it had approximately $850 million in free cash flow, which means that it has lots of money to go out and acquire another company or pay higher dividends or buy back its stock.

Torchmark is a big buyer of its own shares, which Warren loves. From 2000 to 2011, the company has shrunk its outstanding number of shares by 44%. This caused per share earnings to rise over the same period by 188%, while actual net earnings grew by only 38%. The decrease in the number of shares increased the remaining share piece of the net earnings pie. This is one of the benefits of having a very profitable insurance company: It can buy back its own stock and drive up per share earnings by a substantial amount over just a ten-year period of time. This same equation was used by GEICO to help drive up its per share earnings before it was taken over by Berkshire.

PER SHARE EARNINGS HISTORY

Torchmark's per share earnings history shows a strong long-term upward trend. Per share earnings went from $1.27 a share in 1995 to $4.65 a share in 2011.

From 2001 to 2011 Torchmark showed a 124% increase in earnings per share—growing at a compounding annual rate of 8.43% for the last ten years. This means that with an asking price of $36, against earnings of $4.65 a share in 2011, we can argue that we are buying an equity bond that is going to earn an after–corporate tax initial rate of return of 12.9%. Which we can argue is going to grow at an average annual rate of 8.43% over the next ten years.

Year	EPS (Earnings Per Share, $)
'11	4.65
'10	4.27
'09	3.98
'08	3.86
'07	3.63
'06	3.33
'05	3.06
'04	2.82
'03	2.57
'02	2.34
'01	2.07

Per Share Book Value History

From 2001 to 2011 Torchmark showed a 181% increase in per share book value, growing at a compounding annual rate of 10.89% for the last ten years.

Year	BVPS (Book Value Per Share, $)
'11	38.10
'10	33.79
'09	27.35
'08	17.49
'07	24.05
'06	23.50
'05	22.10
'04	21.12
'03	19.16
'02	16.07
'01	13.55

Buffett Buy Analysis

In 2011 Torchmark had a per share book value of $38.10 a
share and was earning approximately $4.65 a share. Which
means that we can argue that as an equity bond, it is earning
an annual rate of return of 12.2%. But in 2011 we can buy it at
BELOW its per share book value of $38.10. That means we can
earn an even higher rate of return: at Torchmark's 2011 market
price of $36 a share, we will be earning an after–corporate tax
initial rate of return on our equity bond of 12.9% ($4.65 ÷ $36
= 12.9%). We can project that the after–corporate tax rate of
return will increase as the company increases its earnings, at its
historic annual per share growth rate of 8.43%.

The next question is what will a $4.65 after–corporate rate of tax return growing at an annual rate of approximately 8.43% look like in ten years? We determine that by using the Future Value Calculator located on the Internet at http://www.investopedia.com/calculator/FVCal.aspx

Plug in: 8.43% for the Interest Rate; $4.65 for the Present Value; and 10 for the number of Time Periods; then click the calculate button and get $10.45. Which means that by 2021, Torchmark will be earning $10.45 a share.

Now what will that $10.45 a share be worth to us in 2021? That all depends on what price-to-earnings ratio the stock market is valuing the stock at in 2021. If it is at its 2011 P/E ratio of 8 (which is near the lowest P/E ratios for the last ten years), we can project that the stock will be trading at approximately $83.60 a share ($10.45 x 8 = $83.60). If we bought Torchmark stock at $36 a share in 2011 and sold it for $83.60 a share in 2021, our total gain on the sale would be $47.60 a share, giving us a total return of 132% and an annual rate of return of 8.79% for the ten-year period.

Torchmark has consistently raised its dividend every year for the last ten years. If it can just maintain its 2011 dividend of $0.49 a share till 2021, we can add $4.90 to our $83.60 gross proceeds from the sale, boosting our proceeds from sale and dividends up to $88.50. The inclusion of the dividends increases our total return to 145% and our annual rate of return to 9.41%.

To run the rate of return equation go to http://www
.moneychimp.com/calculator/discount_rate_calculator.htm
There, put in $36 for the Present Value; $88.50 for the Future
Value; 10 for the Number of Years; then click the calculate
button to get the compounding annual growth rate, which in
this case equals 9.41%.

The question now is does a projected annual rate of return
of 9.41% for ten years seem tantalizing enough for you? For
Warren it is interesting enough to keep $101 million invested
in Torchmark stock.

CHAPTER 19

Union Pacific Corporation

Address:
1416 Dodge Street
Omaha, NE 68179 USA
Telephone: (402) 271-5777
Website: http://www.up.com

Industry: Railroad

Key Statistics:
Public Company
Founded in 1862
Employees: 42,884
Revenue: $18.7 billion (2011)
Net Earnings: $3.2 billion (2011)
Per Share Earnings: $6.50 (2011)
Average Annual Growth for Per Share Earnings: 13.15%
Per Share Book Value: $40.95
Average Annual Growth for Per Share Book Value: 11.19%
Dividend/Yield 2011: $1.90/1.81%
Year of Berkshire Purchase: 2007
Average Per Share Price Berkshire Paid: $50
Stock Exchanges: NYSE
Ticker Symbol: UNP

In May of 2007 Berkshire announced that it had bought 10.5 million Union Pacific shares (about 4% of the total company) at a cost of approximately $50 a share, for a total cost of $525 million. To comply with antitrust regulations, Berkshire sold its position in Union Pacific in 2009, at a profit, when it acquired the Burlington Northern Santa Fe Railroad. With Union Pacific trading at $100 a share in 2011, had Berkshire kept its UP shares, its position would be worth approximately $1.05 billion, which equates to a 100% return on Warren's original investment, in just a little under four years.

Once upon a time Warren owned minority interests in two railroads, the Burlington Northern Santa Fe and the Union Pacific Corporation. When Warren merged Berkshire with the Burlington Northern, he sold off Berkshire's interest in Union Pacific. The reason for Warren selling off the Union Pacific shares? As he said, it had to do with avoiding antitrust problems and getting the government to approve the merger between Berkshire and the Burlington Northern. He didn't want to give the feds even the slightest reason for them to say no to his purchase of Burlington.

We can no longer invest in the Burlington Northern unless we buy shares in Berkshire Hathaway. But we still can invest in Warren's second favorite railroad, the Union Pacific Corporation.

Union Pacific's
Durable Competitive Advantage

In the early 1800s America's railroads had an economic monopoly when it came to the transportation of people and goods in and across America. A true monopoly occurs where there are no competitors. An economic monopoly occurs where there are competitors, but one company is the low-cost provider, which essentially kills the competition. With the railroads there has always been competition; in the early days the railroads competed with steamships on the rivers and wagons on land. The railroad's economic advantage lay in shipping both people and goods over long distances—they could do it faster and more cheaply than the competition.

This economic advantage gave owners of the railroads great wealth and allowed them to consolidate, creating larger economic monopolies and regional monopolies as well. One of the most famous railroad monopolies of this period was the Northwest Securities Corporation. This railroad trust was formed by the consolidation of railroads owned by E. H. Harriman, James J. Hill, J. P. Morgan, and J. D. Rockefeller. These industrial titans realized that if they joined forces and pooled their resources, they would eliminate competition and be able to set prices. This, in turn, allowed them to raise prices and make fantastic sums of money.

These actions made these railroad barons even richer, but the higher prices made the American public feel that they were being taken advantage of. In 1904 Americans got their revenge when President Teddy Roosevelt rode in and broke up the railroad monopolies, splintering the Northwest into a dozen separate railroads, owned by the same railroad barons, who, once again, had to compete with one another.

During the early part of the twentieth century, lots of individual railroads were competing head to head and in the process destroying their profit margins. That, coupled with high capital costs for the track and engines, and a unionized work force, made the railroads poor long-term investments from Warren's perspective.

Then something odd happened, as often does in a competitive world of business: Airlines and trucks emerged as the preferred way for people and goods to travel long distances, and the railroads quickly found themselves struggling for survival against these new competitors.

All this new competition deteriorated the bottom line of the railroads to the point that many were on the verge of bankruptcy. This became a threat to the nation; America, for better or worse, needs its railroads for bulk transportation of raw materials. The United States government came to the rescue by enacting the 1958 Transportation Act, removing the old antitrust laws and once again allowing railroads to consolidate and form regional "rail" monopolies. In 1970 the Supreme Court said the Great Northern, Northern Pacific, Burlington, Spokane, Portland, and Seattle railways could merge to form the Burlington Northern Railway. That company went on to merge with the Atchison, Topeka and Santa Fe Railway in 1996.

To counterbalance the poor economics of the railroads in comparison with trucking operations, the government said that it was okay to consolidate and form regional rail monopolies. Across the industry, small railroads merged with bigger ones to form regional monopolies to compete with trucking.

And then the price of diesel fuel went from 25 cents a gallon in the early 1970s to more than $4 a gallon today, and the economic advantage of shipping by truck suddenly shifted back to shipping by train. Consider these economics: A Union Pacific train can move a ton of freight 865 miles on a single gallon of diesel fuel. This is close to five times more efficient than moving the same cargo by truck and is clearly a long-term cost advantage to the railroads. Add that to the fact that railroads are now able to monopoly-price their services, and you get a very profitable business.

That's the history. Now let's ask some basic questions that Warren uses to identify a company with a durable consumer monopoly.

Will the product or service the company is selling today be the same product or service that it will be selling ten years

from now? In the Union Pacific's case it will probably be the same product and service that it will be selling a hundred years from now.

Does Warren understand how the product works? Yes, you make a product, put the product on a railcar, and the Union Pacific takes it to wherever you want it to go.

Does it take large amounts of research and development to keep the service or product competitive? Railroads do very little research and development—all the technology advancements such as faster and more fuel efficient engines to pull the trains are developed by other companies and then sold to the UP. Even its advances in computing, data processing, and communications were all developed outside the UP by other companies.

Does the company in question have a monopoly or is it the leading low-cost producer of the product or service it sells? Arguably the Union Pacific is both a monopoly and a low-cost producer of the services it provides.

BUSINESS ECONOMICS OF THE UNION PACIFIC

How well has the Union Pacific done over the last ten years? In other words, how big is its competitive advantage? And is that advantage being turned into real bottom-line dollars? Let's run some numbers.

The economic scenario that Warren is arguing is that the underlying economics of these newly minted monopolies are ever improving as their economies of scale improve and they take a bigger and bigger piece of the transport dollar away from trucking. Let's see if the net profit margin of the UP is improving over a ten-year period.

YEAR	NPM (Net Profit Margin, %)
'11	17.1
'10	16.4
'09	12.9
'08	13.0
'07	11.4
'06	10.3
'05	6.7
'04	6.2
'03	9.1
'02	9.0
'01	8.1

We can see that from 2001 to 2011 the Union Pacific saw a little better than a 100% increase in its profit margin, going from 8.1% to 17.1%. How good is a 17.1% profit margin? Consider this: Trucking giant Werner Enterprises consistently delivers a profit margin in the neighborhood of

5%. Meanwhile, industrial and financial giant GE, in good years, shows only a profit margin in the neighborhood of 11%, and Coca-Cola, which has one of most durable competitive advantages ever created, reported a profit margin of 24.1% in 2010. The Union Pacific, a railroad, is starting to generate profit margins that are fast approaching 20%, which are far in excess of what the trucking industry is producing and more in line with a consumer products company like Coca-Cola. Things go better with Coke, but your goods travel better with the Union Pacific.

INCREASE IN BOOK VALUE

While book value is a crude and often inaccurate form of valuation, Warren still looks at increases in book value as a way to determine whether the underlying value of the business is growing. With the Union Pacific we see an increase from $17.47 a share in 2000 to $36.14 a share in 2010, giving the UP a little bit better than a 100% increase in its book value for the ten-year period. Compare that to trucker Werner Enterprises, which showed a 34% increase in its per share book value for the same period. For the record, GE showed a 120% increase and Coca-Cola showed a 215% increase for the same period.

YEAR	BVPS (Book Value Per Share, $)
'11	40.95
'10	36.14
'09	33.54
'08	30.70
'07	29.87
'06	27.74
'05	24.85
'04	22.95
'03	23.93
'02	20.99
'01	19.13

EARNINGS PER SHARE

Let's check out Union Pacific's after–corporate tax earnings per share history.

YEAR	EPS (Earnings Per Share, $)
'11	6.50
'10	5.53
'09	3.61
'08	4.45
'07	3.46
'06	2.96
'05	1.70
'04	1.45

Year	EPS ($)
'03	2.04
'02	2.15
'01	1.89

The Union Pacific's net earnings history shows a strong and consistent upward trend—growing 243%, at an average compounding rate of 13.15% for the last ten years.

Looking at It
from a Business Perspective

In 2011 the Union Pacific had a per share book value of $40.95 and was earning approximately $6.50 a share. This means that we can argue that as an equity bond it is earning an annual rate of return of 15.8%. But we can't buy the stock at its per share book value, we have to pay its 2011 market price of approximately $100 a share. Which means we earn an after–corporate tax rate of return of 6.5% ($6.50 ÷ $100 = 6.5%). We can also project that after–corporate tax rate of return will increase as the company increases its earnings at its historical annual rate of 13.15%.

The next question is what will a $6.50 after–corporate tax rate of return growing at an annual rate of approximately 13.15% look like in ten years? The Future Value Calculator located on the Internet at http://www.investopedia.com/calculator/FVCal.aspx can help us answer that question.

Plug in: 13.1% for the Interest Rate; $6.50 for the Present Value; and 10 for the number of Time Periods; then click the calculate button to get $22.26. Which means that by 2021, Union Pacific will be earning $22.26 a share.

Now what will that $22.26 a share be worth to us in 2021? That all depends on what price-to-earnings ratio the stock market is valuing the stock at in 2021. If it is at its 2011 P/E ratio of 13.8 (which is the lowest P/E ratio for the last ten years), we can project that the stock will be trading at approximately $307.18 a share ($22.26 x 13.8 = $307.18). If we bought Union Pacific stock at $100 a share in 2011 and sold it for $307.18 a share in 2021, our total gain on the sale would be $207.18 a share, giving us a total return of 207% and an annual rate of return of 11.88% for the ten-year period.

Union Pacific has consistently raised its dividend every year for the last ten years. If it can just maintain its 2011 dividend of $1.90 a share till 2021, we can add $19 to our $307.18 gross proceeds from the sale, boosting our proceeds from sale and dividends up to $326.18. The inclusion of the dividends increases our total return to 226% and our annual rate of return to 12.55%.

To run the rate of return equation go to http://www.moneychimp.com/calculator/discount_rate_calculator.htm

There, put in $100 for the Present Value; $326.18 for the Future Value; 10 for the Number of Years; then click the calculate button to get the compounding annual growth rate, which in this case equals 12.55%.

The question now is does a projected annual rate of return of 12.55% for ten years seem attractive to you?

CHAPTER 20

U.S. Bancorp

Address:
800 Nicollet Mall
Minneapolis, MN 55402-4302 USA
Telephone: (651) 466-3000
Website: http://www.usbank.com

Industry: Retail and Commercial Banking

Key Statistics:
Public Company
Founded in 1850
Employees: 63,000
Net Earnings: $4.6 billion (2011)
Per Share Earnings: $2.05 (2011)
Average Annual Growth for Per Share Earnings: 6.11%
Per Share Book Value: $16.45
Average Annual Growth for Per Share Book Value: 10.1%
Dividend/Yield 2011: $0.50/1.85%
Years of Berkshire Purchase: 2006, 2007, 2009
Average Per Share Price Berkshire Paid: $30.75
Stock Exchanges: NYSE
Ticker Symbol: USB

As of 2011 Berkshire owns 78,060,769 shares, or 4.1% of U.S. Bancorp's outstanding shares. With U.S. Bancorp trading at $24 a share, Berkshire's position is worth approximately $1.87 billion; with an average per share cost of $30.75 and a total cost of $2.4 billion, Berkshire has a loss of $530 million due to the market's recent decline—from Buffett's perspective, the declining stock price makes it a better long-term investment, as long as the underlying economics are strong.

U.S. Bancorp is the fifth largest commercial bank in the U.S., with more than $311 billion in assets, and it is the sixth largest bank in the U.S., based on deposits, with $204 billion in deposits. It has over 3,000 banking branch offices and 5,320 ATMs in twenty-five states. U.S. Bancorp offers regional business and consumer banking, wealth management services, national wholesale and trust services, and global payments services to more than 16 million customers.

But what U.S. Bancorp is super good at is growing its business by merging or acquiring other banks. A company that started in 1850 with $8,500 in capital and one teller grew through acquisitions and mergers into the colossus that it has become today. Since 1988 alone, U.S. Bancorp has acquired or merged with over fifty other banks. It has more full-service banking offices in more states than any other bank. In fact, Warren Buffett keeps his $43 billion in Berkshire Hathaway stock certificates tucked away in a U.S. Bancorp safety-deposit box in Omaha, Nebraska.

What Warren finds interesting about U.S. Bancorp is that it really knows how to make money and it knows how to grow through acquisitions that make business sense—which means it doesn't overpay for them. Over the last ten years, it has consistently delivered returns on equity in the 20% range and its return on total assets on average have been in the 2% range, which is the best performance of any of Warren's banking investments.

If we look at U.S. Bancorp's per share earnings history, we can see that from 2001 to 2011 it showed a 55% increase in earnings per share—with only a single losing year in 2009. But overall it grew at a compounding annual rate of 4.5% for the last ten years.

YEAR	EPS (Earnings Per Share, $)
'11	2.05
'10	1.73
'09	0.97
'08	1.61
'07	2.43
'06	2.61
'05	2.42
'04	2.18
'03	1.92
'02	1.84
'01	1.32

With per share earnings in 2011 at $2.05 and an asking price of $24 a share, we can project that we are earning an initial after–corporate tax return of $2.05, or 8.5%; and we can state that that 8.5% initial rate of return will grow at an annual rate of 4.5%.

Per Share Book Value History

From 2001 to 2011 U.S. Bancorp showed a 96% increase in per share book value—and it never had a losing year, growing at a compounding annual rate of 6.9% for the last ten years.

Year	BVPS (Book Value Per Share, $)
'11	16.55
'10	14.78
'09	13.15
'08	10.47
'07	11.60
'06	11.45
'05	11.01
'04	10.52
'03	10.01
'02	9.44
'01	8.43

In 2011 U.S. Bancorp had a per share book value of $16.55 and was earning approximately $2.05 a share. Which means that we can argue that as an equity bond, it is earning an annual rate of return of 12% ($2.05 ÷ $16.55 = 12%).

But we can't buy it at its book value; we have to pay the stock market price, which can significantly alter the economics of our investment. If we pay the 2011 stock market price of approximately $24 a share, we can argue that we are going to be earning an after–corporate tax initial rate of return on our U.S. Bancorp equity bond of 8.5% ($2.05 ÷ $24 = 8.5%). That initial after–corporate tax rate of return will increase as the company increases its earnings, which we are projecting will be at its historic per share annual growth rate of 4.5%. The next question is what will a $2.05 initial after–corporate tax rate of return growing at an annual rate of 4.5% look like in ten years? Let's use the Future Value Calculator located on the Internet at http://www.investopedia.com/calculator/FVCal.aspx

Plug in: 4.5% for the Interest Rate; $2.05 for the Present Value; and 10 for the number of Time Periods; then click the calculate button to get $3.18. Which means that at an annual per share earnings growth rate of 4.5%, by 2021 U.S. Bancorp will be earning $3.18 a share.

Now what will that $3.18 be worth to us in 2021? That all depends on what price-to-earnings ratio the stock market is valuing the stock at in 2021. If it is at its 2011 P/E ratio of 12.3 (its ten-year low), we can project that the stock will be trading at $39.11 a share (12.3 x $3.18 = $39.11). If we bought U.S. Bancorp stock at $24 a share in 2011 and sold it for $39.11 a share in 2021, our total gain from the sale would be $15.11 a share, giving us a total return of 62% and an annual compounding rate of return of 5% for the ten-year period.

Though U.S. Bancorp dropped its dividend in the financial debacle of 2009, in 2011 it is paying a dividend of $0.50 a share. If it can maintain its 2011 dividend of $0.50 a share till 2021, we can add $5 a share (10 x $0.50 = $5) to our $39.11 gross proceeds from the sale, boosting our proceeds from sale and dividends up to $44.11, which increases our total return to 83% and our annual compounding rate of return to 6.28%.

Now the question is, do you find a potential ten-year annual compounding rate of return of 6.28% interesting? Warren found it interesting enough to invest $2.4 billion in the company.

CHAPTER 21

Wal-Mart Stores, Inc.

Address:
702 SW 8th Street
Bentonville, AR 72716 USA
Telephone: (479) 273–4000
Website: http://www.walmartstores.com

Industry: Discount Retail/Groceries/And Just About
Everything Else

Key Statistics:
Public Company
Founded in 1962
Employees: Over 2 million (it's the world's largest private
employer)
Sales: $421 billion (2011)
Net Earnings: $15.3 billion (2011)
Per Share Earnings: $4.45 (2011)
Average Annual Growth for Per Share Earnings: 11.49%
Per Share Book Value: $19.35
Average Annual Growth for Per Share Book Value: 11.19%
Dividend/Yield 2011: $1.46/2.68%
Years of Berkshire Purchase: 2005, 2009
Average Per Share Price Berkshire Paid: $48
Stock Exchanges: NYSE
Ticker Symbol: WMT

As of 2011, Berkshire owns 39,037,142 million shares, or approximately 1.1% of Wal-Mart's outstanding shares. With Wal-Mart trading at $54 a share, Berkshire's position is worth approximately $2.1 billion; with a cost of approximately $1.89 billion, Berkshire has a $210 million profit on this investment.

Wal-Mart Stores, Inc., is the world's largest retailer and the world's largest company by revenue. In America alone it has 2,747 superstores, 803 discount stores, 596 Sam's Clubs, and 158 Neighborhood Markets. Internationally it has over 4,000 stores in Latin America, Asia, Canada, and the UK. All told it has over 8,400 stores in 15 different countries under 55 different names. It operates in Mexico as Walmex, in the United Kingdom as ASDA, in Japan as Seiyu, in Brazil as Bompreco, and in India as Best Price. The company opened its first Supercenter and Sam's Club in Shenzhen, China, in 1996 and now has 189 stores in 101 cities in China. Wal-Mart just acquired 51% of Massmart, the largest general retailer in sub-Sahara Africa. Whether or not he intended it when he opened his first store in 1962, Sam Walton created a retail empire that now spans the globe.

Sam Walton made his name in the discount store business by shaving a few percentage points off his markup, making the difference up with more volume, and giving his customers great service. But the real secret to Wal-Mart's success is the same secret that Mrs. B at the Nebraska Furniture Mart discovered in 1937: Buy in large enough volume and you can get much better prices from your suppliers—who are also hungry for more volume. The result is that NFM and Wal-Mart have lower product costs than their competitors, which means they can offer the customer a bargain price and still have higher margins than the competition. That means they not only get to make more money than the competition, but they also eventually drive their competitors out of business.

What is interesting about this business model is that once it is in place it is very hard for competitors to enter the marketplace because they simply don't have the purchasing power to force suppliers to give them their rock-bottom price. Wal-Mart has the ability to purchase goods at the lowest possible price and then pass part of that savings on to Wal-Mart's customers; the other part is used to grow the business.

Per Share Earnings History

From 2001 to 2011 Wal-Mart showed a 196% increase in earnings per share—and it never had a losing year, growing at an annual rate of 11.49% for the last ten years.

YEAR	EPS (Earnings Per Share, $)
'11	4.45
'10	4.05
'09	3.66
'08	3.42
'07	3.17
'06	2.92
'05	2.63
'04	2.41
'03	2.03
'02	1.81
'01	1.50

With per share earnings in 2011 of $4.45 a share and an asking price of $54 a share, we can argue that we are earning an after–corporate tax initial rate of return of 8.2% ($4.45 ÷ $54 = 8.2%); and say that that 8.2% initial rate of return will grow at an annual rate of 11.49%.

PER SHARE BOOK VALUE HISTORY

From 2001 to 2011, Wal-Mart showed a 188% increase in per share book value—and it never had a losing year, growing at a compounding annual rate of 11.19% for the last ten years—which is a very attractive growth rate.

YEAR	BVPS (Book Value Per Share, $)
'11	19.35
'10	18.80
'09	18.69
'08	16.63
'07	16.26
'06	14.91
'05	12.77
'04	11.67
'03	10.12
'02	8.95
'01	7.88

BUFFETT BUY ANALYSIS

In 2011 Wal-Mart had a per share book value of $19.35 and was earning approximately $4.45 a share. This means that as an equity bond, it is earning an annual rate of return of 22% ($4.45 ÷ $19.35 = 22%).

We can't buy Wal-Mart at its per share book value, $19.35. We have to pay the stock market price in 2011 of approximately $54 a share, which means we can argue that we are going to be earning an after–corporate tax initial rate of return on our Wal-Mart equity bond of 8.2% ($4.45 ÷ $54 = 8.2%). That initial after–corporate tax rate of return will increase as the company increases its earnings, which we are projecting will be at its historic per share annual growth rate of 11.49%.

To answer the question, what will a $4.45 after–corporate tax rate of return growing at an annual rate of approximately 11.49% look like in ten years, we need to use the Future Value Calculator located on the Internet at http://www.investopedia.com/calculator/FVCal.aspx

Plug in: 11.49% for the Interest Rate Per Time Period; $4.45 for the Present Value; and 10 for the number of Time Periods; then click the calculate button and get $13.20. Which means that by 2021 Wal-Mart will be earning approximately $13.20 a share.

Now what will that $13.20 or 24.4% return be worth to us in 2021? That all depends on what price-to-earnings ratio the stock market is valuing the stock at in 2021. If the stock is at its 2011 P/E ratio of 13 (the ten-year low), we can project that it will be trading at approximately $171.60 a share ($13.20 x 13 = $171.60). If we bought Wal-Mart stock at $54 a share in 2011 and sold it for $171.60 a share in 2021, our total gain on the sale would be $117.60 a share, giving us a total return of 217% and an annual rate of return of 12.26% for the ten-year period.

Wal-Mart has consistently raised its dividend every year for the last seventeen years. If it can maintain its 2011 dividend of $1.48 a share till 2021, we can add $14.80 to our $171.60

proceeds from the sale, boosting our gross proceeds from sale and dividends up to $186.40, which increases our total return up to 238% and our annual rate of return to 13.19%.

To run the rate of return equation go to http://www.moneychimp.com/calculator/discount_rate_calculator.htm Then put in $54 for the Present Value; $186.40 for the Future Value; 10 for the Number of Years; and click the calculate button to get the compounding annual growth rate, which in this case equals 13.19%.

Is a projected annual rate of return of 13.19% for ten years interesting enough for you? For Warren it is interesting enough to keep $2.14 billion of his money tied up in Wal-Mart stock.

CHAPTER 22

Washington Post Company

Address:
1150 15th Street, NW
Washington, DC 20071 USA
Telephone: (202) 334-6000
Website: http://www.washpostco.com

Industry: Newspaper Publishing, TV Stations, Cable

Key Statistics:
Public Company
Founded in 1877
Employees: 20,000
Sales: $4.7 billion (2011)
Net Earnings: $200 million (2011)
Per Share Earnings: $34.75 (2011)
Average Annual Growth for Per Share Earnings: 8.39%
Per Share Book Value: $427
Average Annual Growth for Per Share Book Value: 9.59%
Dividend/Yield 2011: $9.40/2.78%
Years of Berkshire Purchase: 1973, 1974
Average Per Share Price Berkshire Paid: $6.36
Stock Exchanges: NYSE
Ticker Symbol: WPO

As of 2011, Berkshire owns 1,727,765 shares, or 18.2% of Washington Post's outstanding shares. With Washington Post trading at $338 a share, Berkshire's position is worth approximately $583 million; with a cost of $11 million or $6.36 a share, Berkshire has a profit of approximately $572 million on this investment.

The Washington Post Company, besides owning a leading U.S. newspaper (daily circ. 615,628), also owns the *Herald* newspaper in Everett, Washington. Also on its list of money-making assets are six network-affiliated TV stations and numerous small cable TV companies in rural markets across nineteen states (700,000 subscribers). It also owns Kaplan Inc., which teaches people how to study for a long list of school and professional exams.

The bottom line here is that the Washington Post Company has lots of ways to make money, which is a good thing because newspapers are fast becoming a thing of the past due to the Internet. But they aren't dead yet, and combined with Washington Post's other assets, media are still a money-making machine.

Even with advertising in a recession-induced slump, the Washington Post Company is on track to earn, after corporate tax, a net profit of $275 million in 2011, which is approximately 83% of what it was making at the top of the bubble in 2006. But notice this: In 2005 it reported net earnings of $32.59 a share on a total net profit of $314 million, but in 2011 it reported net earnings of $34.75 a share on a total net profit of $275 million. Make less money, but report an increase in per share earnings? How is that possible?

It's done through the magic of share repurchases. The Washington Post, like clockwork, has been buying back the number of shares it has outstanding—from 9.60 million in 2005 to 7.75 million in 2011—a 19.2% decline in the number of shares outstanding, which has the overall effect of driving up per share earnings. Let me show you: Take the 2005 net profit of $314.3 million and divide it by the 9.6 million shares the company had outstanding in 2005, and you get earnings of $32.70 a share ($314 million ÷ 9.6 million = $32.70). But take the 2005 net profit of $314.3 million and divide it by the number of shares outstanding in 2011, which was 7.75 million, and you get $40.55 a share ($314.3 million ÷ 7.75 million = $40.55). Decrease the number of shares outstanding and increase the per share earnings.

Which is how the Washington Post Company, doing business in two very mature areas—newspapers and television—can keep driving up its per share earnings even in periods when net profits are slowly declining.

Warren's initial investment in the Washington Post Company cost him a grand total of $11 million, at $6.36 a share, back in 1973–1974. Thirty-seven years later, in 2011, the Washington Post is earning an after–corporate tax rate of return of $34.75 a share, which gives Warren's Washington Post equity bonds, in 2011, an after–corporate tax annual yield of 546%. On a $6.36-a-share investment back in 1973–1974, with the stock trading at $338 in 2011, Warren can calculate a total return of 5,214%, which equates to an 11.34% annual compounding rate of return for the 37-year period. Which is about as good as it gets.

But this isn't 1974 and we aren't going to buy the Washington Post at $6 a share; we are going to have to pay $338 a share. So the question is this: If we buy the Washington Post at $338 a share in 2011, how are we going to do? To figure that out let's do the Buffett buy analysis.

BUFFETT BUY ANALYSIS

If we look at Washington Post's per share earnings history we can see that from 2000 to 2011 it showed a 142% increase in earnings per share and an overall annual compounding growth rate of 8.39% for the last eleven years. (Please note: We use eleven years here instead of ten. The reason for this is that the recession of 2001 produced lower-than-normal earnings in the advertising industry. If we use 2001 as a base year for our valuation calculations, we will be generating an abnormally high per share earnings growth rate, which will give us very high future valuations that are out of line with the underlying economics of the business. But this also tells us that a recession is a good time to buy shares in the Washington Post, as the recession creates momentary setbacks in its earnings that usually result in a lower stock price over the short term.)

YEAR	EPS (Earnings Per Share, $)
'11	34.75
'10	34.26
'09	9.78 Recession
'08	19.22
'07	30.19
'06	34.74
'05	32.70
'04	34.59
'03	19.08
'02	22.10
'01	7.54 Recession
'00	14.32

With Washington Post's per share earnings in 2011 at $34.75 and an asking price of $338 a share, we can argue that we are earning an initial rate of return of $34.75 a share, or 10.2% ($34.75 ÷ $338 = 10.2%); and we can say that that 10.2% initial rate of return will grow at an annual rate of 8.39%.

Per Share Book Value History

From 2000 to 2011 Washington Post showed a 173% increase in per share book value—growing at a compounding annual rate of 9.59% for the last eleven years.

Year	BVPS (Book Value Per Share, $)
'11	427.00
'10	342.00
'09	315.00
'08	303.00
'07	362.00
'06	330.00
'05	274.00
'04	251.00
'03	216.00
'02	193.00
'01	177.00
'00	156.00

In 2011 Washington Post had a per share book value of $427 and was earning approximately $34.75 a share. Which means that we can argue that as an equity bond, it is earning an annual rate of return of 8.1%, which we can argue is going to grow at Washington Post's per share earnings annual growth rate of 8.39%.

But here we can buy it at below its per share book value, $427. We get to pay the stock market price in 2011 of approximately $338 a share. This means we can argue that we are going to be earning 10.27%. And that is an even better initial rate of return, which, we can argue, will increase on an annual basis at a rate of 8.39%.

To help us determine what a $34.75 initial rate of return growing at an annual rate of 8.39% will look like in ten years? We can use the Future Value Calculator located on the Internet at http://www.investopedia.com/calculator/FVCal .aspx

Plug in: 8.39% for the Interest Rate Per Time Period; $34.75 for the Present Value; and 10 for the number of Time Periods; then click the calculate button to get $77.78. Which means Washington Post stock by 2021 will be earning $77.78 a share.

Now what will that $77.78 be worth to us in 2021? That all depends on what price-to-earnings ratio the stock market is valuing the stock at in 2021. If it is at its 2011 P/E ratio of 12.5 (its lowest P/E in fifteen years), then we can project that the stock will be trading at $972.25 a share (12.5 x $77.78 = $972.25). If we bought Washington Post stock at $338 a share in 2011 and sold it for $972.25 a share in 2021, our total gain from the sale would be $634.25 a share, giving us a total return of 187% and an annual rate of return of 11.14% for the ten-year period.

Though the Washington Post Company has consistently raised its dividend over the last ten years, if it can just maintain its 2011 dividend of $9.40 a share till 2021, we can add $94 to our $972.25 gross proceeds from the sale, boosting our proceeds from sale and dividends up to $1,066.25, which increases our total return to 215% and our annual rate of return to 12.17%.

The question now is, does a projected annual rate of return of 12.17% for ten years interest you? For Warren it is interesting enough to keep $394 million worth of Washington Post stock on his books.

CHAPTER 23

Wells Fargo & Company

Address:
420 Montgomery Street
San Francisco, CA 94104 USA
Telephone: (800) 292-9932
Website: http://www.wellsfargo.com

Industry: Retail and Commercial Banking

Key Statistics:
Public Company
Founded in 1852
Employees: 267,300
Net Earnings: $15.5 billion (2011)
Per Share Earnings: $2.85 (2011)
Average Annual Growth for Per Share Earnings: 11.15%
Per Share Book Value: $22.45
Average Annual Growth for Per Share Book Value: 11.19%
Dividend/Yield 2011: $0.48/1.65%
Years of Berkshire Purchase: 1989, 1990, 1998, 2005,
    2008, 2009, 2010
Average Per Share Price Berkshire Paid: $22.32
Stock Exchanges: NYSE
Ticker Symbol: WFC

As of 2011, Berkshire owns 358,936,125 shares, or 6.8% of Wells Fargo's outstanding shares. With Wells Fargo trading at $28 a share, Berkshire's position is worth approximately $10 billion; with an average per share cost of $22.32 and a total cost of $8.015 billion, Berkshire has a profit of $2 billion on this investment.

Buffett's stake in Wells Fargo: Warren initially bought 5 million shares for $289.4 million during the banking crisis of 1989–1990. Over the next twenty years, with the help of stock splits and additional investments, he increased his position to 358.9 million shares worth approximately $10 billion. He has been actively buying more of WFC stock during the recent banking crisis, adding to his position in 2008, 2009, and 2010. It is his second largest stockholding after Coca-Cola.

Wells Fargo was founded in 1852 by Henry Wells and William G. Fargo, the two founders of American Express, to provide banking services to the gold rush state of California, which was awash in newfound wealth. Through a series of mergers and buyouts over its 159-year history, it grew into the second largest bank in the U.S. by assets. For many years it was the only U.S. bank to hold the coveted S&P AAA rating, which during the 2008 financial crisis was downgraded to AA-, where it still remains. During the 2008 financial crisis it was one of the few banks that actually reported a net profit. Warren considers Wells Fargo to be the best-run large bank in America.

Warren took his first position during the 1989–1990 real estate crash, which decimated banking stocks. He had the cash to do it and when the fund managers of the world were running from banking stocks, Warren stepped up to the plate and invested heavily in Wells Fargo.

This is what Warren had to say when he made the investment:

> With Wells Fargo, we think we have obtained the best managers in the business, Carl Reichardt and Paul Hazen. In many ways the combination of Carl and Paul reminds me of another—Tom Murphy and Dan Burke at Capital Cities/ABC. First, each pair is stronger than the sum of its parts because each partner understands, trusts and admires the other. Second, both managerial teams pay able people well, but abhor having a bigger head count than is needed. Third, both attack costs as vigorously when profits are at record levels as when they are under pressure. Finally, both stick with what they understand and let their abilities, not their egos, determine what they attempt. (Thomas J. Watson Sr. of IBM followed the same rule: "I'm no genius," he said. "I'm smart in spots—but I stay around those spots.")
>
> Our purchases of Wells Fargo in 1990 were helped by a chaotic market in bank stocks. The disarray was appro-

priate: Month by month the foolish loan decisions of once well-regarded banks were put on public display. As one huge loss after another was unveiled—often on the heels of managerial assurances that all was well—investors understandably concluded that no bank's numbers were to be trusted. Aided by their flight from bank stocks, we purchased our 10% interest in Wells Fargo for $290 million, less than five times after-tax earnings and less than three times pre-tax earnings.

Wells Fargo is big—it has $56 billion in assets—and has been earning more than 20% on equity and 1.25% on assets. Our purchase of one-tenth of the bank may be thought of as roughly equivalent to our buying 100% of a $5 billion bank with identical financial characteristics. But were we to make such a purchase, we would have to pay about twice the $290 million we paid for Wells Fargo. Moreover, that $5 billion bank, commanding a premium price, would present us with another problem: We would not be able to find a Carl Reichardt to run it. In recent years, Wells Fargo executives have been more avidly recruited than any others in the banking business; no one, however, has been able to hire the dean. . . .

Consider some mathematics: Wells Fargo currently earns well over $1 billion pre-tax annually after expensing more than $300 million for loan losses. If 10% of all $48 billion of the bank's loans—not just its real estate loans—

were hit by problems in 1991, and these produced losses (including foregone interest) averaging 30% of principal, the company would roughly break even.

A year like that—which we consider only a low-level possibility, not a likelihood—would not distress us. In fact, at Berkshire we would love to acquire businesses or invest in capital projects that produced no return for a year, but that could then be expected to earn 20% on growing equity. Nevertheless, fears of a California real estate disaster similar to that experienced in New England caused the price of Wells Fargo stock to fall almost 50% within a few months during 1990. Even though we had bought some shares at the prices prevailing before the fall, we welcomed the decline because it allowed us to pick up many more shares at the new, panic prices.

Investors who expect to be ongoing buyers of investments throughout their lifetimes should adopt a similar attitude toward market fluctuations; instead many illogically become euphoric when stock prices rise and unhappy when they fall.

So the "trick" is to buy Wells Fargo when the rest of the world doesn't want it. Which Warren has been doing in 2008, 2009, and 2010. And since the market is still low in 2011, we can bet he is still in there buying. Let's look at the numbers and the argument and see where our buying points are.

To start with, let's extend Warren's argument for buying Wells Fargo during the banking crisis of 1990 out to 2011. Wells Fargo in 2011 has an asset base that has grown to $1.32 trillion and after-tax net earnings of $15.5 billion. If Wells Fargo were to see 10% of all of its loans ($132 billion) get into trouble and were those troubled loans to produce a loss of 30% of the principle (approximately $32 billion), it would take Wells Fargo a little over two years' worth of net earnings ($15.5 x 2 = $31 billion) to make up for the loss. In 2011 Wells Fargo estimated that its lone losses would be in the neighborhood of $14 billion, well within the comfort level of one year's after-tax net earnings.

Let's look at some other numbers for Wells Fargo to see if it is a business in 2011 that we might want to own for the long term.

Per Share Earnings History

From 2001 to 2011, Wells Fargo over the last ten years has grown its per share earnings 187%, at a compounding annual rate of 11.15%.

Year	EPS (Earnings Per Share, $)
'11	2.85
'10	2.21
'09	1.75
'08	0.70
'07	2.38
'06	2.49
'05	2.25
'04	2.05
'03	1.83
'02	1.66
'01	0.99

With per share earnings in 2011 at $2.85 and an asking price of $28 a share, we can argue that we are earning an after–corporate tax initial rate of return of $2.85 a share, or 10.1%; and we can say that that 10.1% initial rate of return will grow at an annual rate of 11.15%.

PER SHARE BOOK VALUE HISTORY

From 2001 to 2011, Wells Fargo has grown its per share book value by 188%, at an average annual compounding rate of 11.19%.

YEAR	BVPS (Book Value Per Share, $)
'11	22.45
'10	22.33
'09	19.94
'08	16.02
'07	14.31
'06	13.47
'05	11.61
'04	10.83
'03	9.86
'02	8.67
'01	7.77

Buffett Buy Analysis

In 2011 Wells Fargo had a per share book value of $22.45 a share and was earning approximately $2.85 a share. Which means that we can argue that as an equity bond, it is earning an annual rate of return of 12.6%, which we can argue is going to grow at Wells Fargo's per share earnings annual growth rate of approximately 11.15%.

In 2011 we can't buy it at its per share book value of $22.45, but we can get close. If we pay the 2011 stock market price of approximately $28 a share, we can argue that we are going to be earning an after–corporate tax initial rate of return on our Wells Fargo equity bond of $2.85 a share, or

10.1% ($2.85 ÷ $28 = 10.1%). But that initial after–corporate tax rate of return will increase as the company increases its earnings, which we are projecting will be at its historic annual rate of 11.15%.

The next question is, what will a $2.85 initial after–corporate tax rate of return growing at an annual rate of approximately 11.15% look like in ten years? To help us determine this future value, let's use the Future Value Calculator located on the Internet at http://www.investopedia.com/calculator/FVCal.aspx

Plug in: 11.15% for the Interest Rate Per Time Period; $2.85 for the Present Value; and 10 for the number of Time Periods; then click the calculate button to get $8.20. Which means that if we pay $28 for a share of Wells Fargo stock, by 2021 it will be earning $8.20 a share, which equates to a 29.2% rate of return on our $28-a-share investment.

Now what will that $8.20 be worth to us in 2021? That all depends on what price-to-earnings ratio the stock market is valuing the stock at in 2021. If it is at its 2011 P/E ratio of approximately 12.7 (its historic low), we can project that the stock will be trading at $104.14 a share (12.7 x $8.20 = $104.14).

If we bought Wells Fargo at $28 a share in 2011 and sold it for $104.14 a share in 2021, our total profit on the sale would be $76.14 a share, giving us a total return of 271% and an annual rate of return of 14.04% for the ten-year period.

Though Wells Fargo dropped its dividend in the financial debacle of 2009, in 2011 it is paying a dividend of $0.48 a share. If it can just maintain its 2011 dividend of $0.48 a share till 2021, we can add $4.80 to our $104.14 gross proceeds from the sale, boosting our proceeds from sale and dividends to $108.94, which increases our total return to 289% and our annual rate of return to 14.55%.

Now the question is, does a projected ten-year compounding annual rate of return of 14.55% interest you? Warren finds it interesting enough not only to have invested $8 billion in the company, he also makes a point to buy even more stock whenever the market takes a hit, driving Wells Fargo's stock into a buying range that offers him an attractive rate of return.

CHAPTER 24

Munger, Combs, and Weschler

Berkshire Hathaway's stock portfolio includes investments that are attributed to Charlie Munger, Warren's partner, and to Berkshire's newly hired portfolio managers Todd Combs and Ted Weschler, who now assist Warren in managing a portion of Berkshire's portfolio. Their investments are different from Warren's, and, as such, we thought it wise to discuss them separately.

Charlie Munger

Charlie Munger's primary influence on Warren's investment decisions has been as an advisor. However, there have been a few times when Munger alone has come up with an idea and has pushed Warren to make the investment even though it falls outside the "circle of confidence" that Warren is normally comfortable investing in. Such was Berkshire's investment in BYD Company Ltd.

BYD

Website: http://www.byd.com.cn
BYD trades in China under the symbol:
  002594.SZ (http://www.reuters.com/finance/stocks
  /overview?symbol=002594.SZ).
BYD trades on the Hong Kong Exchange under the symbol: HKG:1211 (http://www.marketwatch.com/investing
  /stock/1211?countrycode=hk).
In the U.S. BYD trades over the counter as an ADR at:
  BYDDY.PK (Berkshire's shares are not ADRs).

As of 2011, Berkshire owns 225 million shares, or 9.9%
of BYD's outstanding shares, which it purchased in 2008
for $232 million, or $1.03 a share. With BYD Company
Ltd. trading in China at the equivalent of US$3.63 a share,
Berkshire's position is worth approximately $816.7 mil-
lion.

Munger considers BYD's founder and chairman Wang
Chuanfu to be "a combination of Thomas Edison and Jack
Welch—something like Edison in solving technical problems,
and something like Welch in getting done what he needs to do.
I have never seen anything like it." Munger liked BYD so much
that he invested approximately $25 million of his own money
in the company, then started lobbying Warren to buy into it.

Charlie Munger was also impressed with the company's
history. Chuanfu started the company in 1995 with

US$300,000 that he borrowed from relatives, with the sole purpose of manufacturing rechargeable batteries to compete with imports manufactured by Sony and Sanyo. Within five years BYD had become large enough to compete on a global scale, and made the leap into designing and manufacturing cell phone handsets for Motorola, Nokia, and Samsung.

In 2003 BYD bought a Chinese state-owned car company that was on the verge of bankruptcy, and by 2008 its F3 model sedan was the best-selling car in China. BYD is now integrating its battery technology into its auto business to build electric cars. BYD employs 130,000 people, with eight factories in China and one each in India, Hungary, and Romania.

How are the economics? They were good. In 2010 BYD earned $0.17 a share, had a gross profit margin of 19%, and a return on equity of 14%. But in the first half of 2011, BYD saw a 90% drop in its net earnings after a decline in auto sales. It is difficult to create a durable competitive advantage in the auto industry in both America and China. But Charlie is a big believer in the vision of the company's founder, so Berkshire continues to hold the stock.

TODD COMBS

Todd Combs is a money manager and potential candidate to succeed Warren as Berkshire's CEO. Since he was hired in

January 2011, he has made investments in MasterCard and Dollar General.

MasterCard

Website: http://www.mastercard.com
Trading Symbol NYSE: MA

As of 2011, Berkshire owns 200,000 shares, which it purchased in the period in 2011 for approximately $46 million, or $233 a share. In the fall of 2011 MasterCard is trading at $323 a share, making Berkshire's position worth approximately $64.6 million.

MasterCard shows all the signs of having a durable competitive advantage. It has high returns on both equity (37%) and capital (37%) and carries zero long-term debt. While it has been in business since 1965, it became a public company only in 2006. Its per share earnings have grown at an annual rate of 21% over the last four years. Its per share book value has been growing at an annual rate of 19.5% over the last four years. It has also been a big buyer of its own stock.

In 2011 MasterCard will report per share earnings of approximately $17.50 a share, with an asking price of $323 a share. Therefore, we get an initial after–corporate tax rate of return of 5.4%. If we project that MasterCard can keep its earnings growing at an annual rate of 21% for the next ten years, we are looking at 2021 earnings of $117 a share. Using the historic low P/E of 16, we can predict that MasterCard in 2021 will be trading at $1,872 a share. If we buy MasterCard in 2011 at $323 a share and sell in 2021 at $1,872 a share, we will be earning a compounding annual rate of return of 19.25%. Even if MasterCard can perform half this well—and grow its earnings at the annual rate of 10%—it will produce a compounding rate of return of 8.93% over the next ten years.

Dollar General Corporation

Website: http://www.dollargeneral.com
Trading Symbol NYSE: DG

As of 2011, Berkshire owns 1,500,000, which it purchased in the second quarter of 2011 for approximately $46.5 million, or $31 a share. In the fall of 2011 Dollar General is trading at $36 a share, making Berkshire's position worth approximately $54 million.

Dollar General stores are the Wal-Mart of towns too small for a Wal-Mart store—or any town under 20,000 people. Presently, there are 9,496 Dollar Stores spread out across small-town America. The company has been in business since 1955 and has such a strong cash flow that it was taken private by an investment group headed by Kohlberg, Kravis, & Roberts in 2007. This same investment group took it public in 2009.

What is particularly attractive about Dollar General is that its gross margin (34%), operating margin (11%), and net profit margin (5.3%) are better than both Wal-Mart's—GM (26%), OM (7.5%), NPM (3.5%)—and Costco's—GM (13%), OM (3.9%), NPM (1.7%). Dollar General's sales are $14.6 billion, which is but a fraction of Wal-Mart's $445 billion and Costco's $85 billion, but sometimes small is better when it comes to making money.

When Dollar General was taken private, it was loaded up with a lot of debt, which the company is busy paying off. This task is made easier because the company does not pay a dividend.

In 2011 Dollar General will report per share earnings of approximately $2.25 a share, with an asking price of $36 a share. This gives us an initial after–corporate tax rate of return of 6.2%. If we project that Dollar General can keep its earnings growing at a historic annual rate of return of 13% for the next ten years, 2021 earnings will be $7.64 a share. Using the historic low P/E of 14, we can predict that Dollar General in 2021 will be trading at $106.96 a share (14 x $7.64 = $106.96). If we buy Dollar General in 2011 at $36 a share and sell in 2021 at $106.96 a share, we will earn a compounding annual rate of return of 11.5% for the ten years we held the investment.

While Todd Combs is not Warren Buffett, he is showing some very Buffett-like investment choices in his first year with Berkshire—both MasterCard and Dollar General have economic pictures that suggest that they benefit from having some kind of durable competitive advantage. We expect to be writing more about Combs and his stock picks in the future.

TED WESCHLER

Ted Weschler is new to the Berkshire team, officially joining in early 2012. His hedge fund, Peninsula Capital Advisors, which he started in 1999, has grown at an average annual rate of 26% for the last eleven years. No small feat given that this includes the worst recession since the Great Depression. If Warren were to look into a mirror that took thirty years off his age, he might see Ted. Gifted with a great intellect, Ted, like Warren, is obsessed with reading corporate annual reports, running a concentrated portfolio, and holding investments for long periods of time. But unlike Warren, he shorts stocks—something that Warren stopped doing in his twenties because the upside risk is limitless. Since, at the writing of this book, Ted has yet to start his new job, we can't report on the investments he will choose for Berkshire. We can, however, speculate that if he continues on with his past performance, Berkshire shareholders are going to be very, very happy.

In Closing

We hope that you have enjoyed this examination of Warren Buffett's stock portfolio. As we said in the beginning, we benefit here from Warren having already identified these businesses as being companies that have a durable competitive advantage. If you would like to know more about being able to identify a company with a durable competitive advantage, we suggest you read our books *The New Buffettology* and *Warren Buffett and the Interpretation of Financial Statements*.

If you have specific questions about this book or Buffett's investment strategy, please feel free to contact us at marybuffettology@gmail.com or davidbuffettology@gmail.com, and we periodically offer Buffettology Investment seminars through Buffettologyseminars.com.

Happy hunting.

MB & DC

Index

215

217

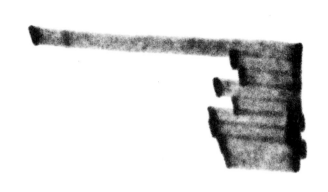